Debt Recovery

How to Overcome Debt and Build Wealth for Life

(The Battle Scarred Guide to Small Business Debt Relief and Recovery)

Lorenzo Harley

Published By **Darby Connor**

Lorenzo Harley

All Rights Reserved

Debt Recovery: How to Overcome Debt and Build Wealth for Life (The Battle Scarred Guide to Small Business Debt Relief and Recovery)

ISBN 978-1-77485-748-9

No part of this guidebook shall be reproduced in any form without permission in writing from the publisher except in the case of brief quotations embodied in critical articles or reviews.

Legal & Disclaimer

The information contained in this ebook is not designed to replace or take the place of any form of medicine or professional medical advice. The information in this ebook has been provided for educational & entertainment purposes only.

The information contained in this book has been compiled from sources deemed reliable, and it is accurate to the best of the Author's knowledge; however, the Author cannot guarantee its accuracy and validity and cannot be held liable for any errors or omissions. Changes are periodically made to this book. You must consult your doctor or get professional medical advice before using any of the suggested remedies, techniques, or information in this book.

Upon using the information contained in this book, you agree to hold harmless the Author from and against any damages, costs, and expenses, including any legal fees potentially resulting from the application of any of the information provided by this guide. This disclaimer applies to any damages or injury caused by the use and application, whether directly or indirectly, of any advice or information presented, whether for breach of contract, tort, negligence, personal injury, criminal intent, or under any other cause of action.

You agree to accept all risks of using the information presented inside this book. You need to consult a professional medical practitioner in order to ensure you are both able and healthy enough to participate in this program.

TABLE OF CONTENTS

Introduction 1

Chapter 1: What Is A Credit Score? ..3

Chapter 2: What Is The Role Of Credit Scores 6

Chapter 3: Why Having A Great Credit Score Is Critical......................12

Chapter 4: What Is The Factor That Determines Your Credit Score 17

Chapter 5: Estimating Your Credit Score...25

Chapter 6: Understanding What Could Damage Your Credit Score....32

Chapter 7: Tips To Enhance Your Credit Score 44

Chapter 8: How Does My Score Influences My Score? 63

Chapter 9: 14 Of The Most Destructive Items On Your Credit Report...95

Chapter 10: Repairing Your Self-Credit Step And Strategies............105

Chapter 11: Perhaps You Have A Need For A Credit Expert...............132

Conclusion 182

Introduction

This book is packed with tested strategies and steps on how to swiftly and effectively repair the credit rating.

Your credit score can affect your life in a variety of ways. Financially, it determines whether or not someone will lend you money. In addition, it also impacts the conditions for the loan.

It doesn't end at this. Your credit score could have an influence on whether an employer will hire you for an employment opportunity and can also affect the housing options you have. In the event of obtaining a loan to purchase the house or get the approval for your rental are influenced on your score.

A higher credit score will increase your odds of getting loans that has an extended repayment time as well as low interest. It can also enhance the chances for you to get a job or housing.

In this book we break it all into pieces. We discuss what is a credit score and what is involved in generating it. We also examine what could be affecting your credit score, and what you can do to correct it fast. You'll be able to start making the necessary adjustments to boost your credit score in the shortest time of reading this book.

I hope you enjoy it!

Chapter 1: What Is A Credit Score?

Your credit score may be the most significant publicly accessible indicator of your financial health. It informs potential lenders or employer in a glance the degree to which you are responsible (or whether or) you make use of credit.

In simple terms the simplest terms, a credit score is a number which demonstrates the creditworthiness of a consumer. Your credit score is an amount that ranges from 300 to 850. From the lender's point of point of view, the better you score is the more appealing an applicant you are.

Who decides on your credit score?

There are many credit scoring methods that are available. Each one is unique to the company who developed it, and utilizes a different method to determine the score of your credit.

As we'll see a little bit later, several factors go into determining your credit score. Each of them contributes a particular proportion of the final score you're given. It can vary based on the scoring method used however, the variables tend to be the same for every model.

It is, in the end, is YOU who determines your score on credit. It's all about whether you've taken out credit previously and, if so it's how carefully you've used it.

What are the Credit Scores used To

Credit scores are an indicator that reflects your overall financial condition. It isn't affected by outside entities (save for the actual financial details pertaining to your personal situation) and is independent. Credit scores are private information that is not accessible to everyone and anyone who has access to Google search. Be assured that your personal credit history isn't moving around on over the Internet unless you decide to make it available publicly.

Be aware that if someone not you has access to your personal information to establish you credit rating without permission You may take legal action. You can file a lawsuit for $1000 or for actual damage incurred, which is more.

A credit score may, however, be used by legitimate parties whenever it is necessary. Therefore, it can be (and generally is) utilized by a variety of organizations and institutions to decide whether to provide you with the services they offer or not.

The credit scores of your clients are analyzed whenever you apply for a type of loan. This includes anything from loans for students to home and auto loans. Insurance companies, potential employers landlords, utility firms also have access to the information. So do several government agencies. They can utilize it to find your contact information, figure out whether you are entitled to unclaimed income and determine how much you are able to pay for child support and more.

Your credit rating is utilized to judge the degree of a worthy (or true) an individual credit card holder you are. Prospective lenders and companies use it to assess the risk they can take on you as a potential borrower. Legal entities can utilize it to decide how they can take appropriate action in line with the law applicable to you.

Chapter 2: What Is The Role Of Credit Scores

The most important factor to improving your credit score is understanding the components of it and how it operates. If you are able to reduce it into elements, you can take on each of them separately. It is easier to comprehend what's going on which direction, and the most efficiently and quickly to alter things to make things better.

How Do Credit Scores Get Created?

There are many different scoring systems that are available currently. Each of them uses its own unique algorithm and approach to things in a unique way. Each business or organization chooses which method to utilize. In some instances they will examine your credit score by a variety of systems prior to making an assessment.

FICO scores are the most widely utilized, with more than 90 percent of credit institutions using FICO scores. Data analytics firm FICO (formerly Fair Isaac Corporation) has not revealed its unique algorithm that calculates scores. It is however known that the formula has five key components, all being weighted in accordance with the importance.

As I've previously mentioned, FICO's system isn't the only acceptable score calculation method available. There are a variety of other options. Because of differences in the methods of calculation the score can vary by up to 100 points from one system to the next system.

Commonly used Scoring Systems for Scoring

We've previously discussed the FICO score as the most popular scoring method. FICO utilizes a variety of scoring algorithms, and each created for a specific use. The NextGen score model for instance is used to determine the risk of credit to consumers and FICO SBSS is used to evaluate the risk of small businesses. FICO SBSS helps assess small-sized businesses that apply for credit.

FICO is based on three credit bureaus across the nation for the calculation of credit scores. These include Experian, Equifax, and TransUnion. These credit bureaus might possess different data on any particular consumer.

The three bureaus mentioned above trying to beat FICO they came together to develop the credit score system of their own. The system is referred to as VantageScore It differs from FICO in many ways. A credit report compiled using VantageScore could show drastically different results than one created using FICO was employed.

Although it isn't as popular in the same way as FICO, VantageScore is also widely accepted by the financial industry. Certain financial institutions look up data from the two systems to consumers prior to making a final decision.

There are various other scoring systems that are available. CE Score is published by CE analytics. The score is currently accessible to over 6000 lending institutions in the U.S.

Most often financial institutions might choose to use credit scores that are not traditional to get a better understanding of their clients. The majority the scores are built upon data that are not accessible to nationwide credit bureaus. The credit scores of these scores can be based more heavily on rental, utility and telecom payments information. Public records information like the mortgage, deeds to property and tax records could also be considered.

Values of Credit Scores

Every each time you calculate your credit score and analyzed, it will be recalculated with a certain number. The range for these scores is dependent on the scoring system employed. FICO as well as VantageScore 4.0 (the most recent VantageScore version) both calculate scores between 300 and 800. Other scoring systems offer completely various scoring options.

In general, however it is true that one thing is common in all models that is the more you rating, the higher it is for you. While no calculation system is flawless, lending institutions continue to view customers who have higher scores as being less risky. This makes them more likely to provide their services, and also get you a better price.

Since FICO is the most frequently used credit score that we'll take an in-depth review of the way their credit ranges are broken down. FICO Score 9: The FICO score 9 is their latest however, numerous institutions still use FICO

8 as their FICO 8 version, and we'll go over the FICO 8 model below.

FICO Scores 8 ranges, and how Lenders Consider These Scores

SCORE RANGE CLASSIFICATION

300-559 Poor

560-669 Fair

670-739 Good

740-799 Very Excellent

800-850 Excellent

How Do Credit Scores Are Calculated

The credit score you receive is based on the elements taken into consideration when formulating it. They will differ significantly between various scoring systems, as well as across different scoring models in this system.

FICO and VantageScore both employ various scoring methods, depend on information provided by the three credit bureaus that are national. This is Equifax, Experian, and TransUnion. Other, less conventional scoring systems could use only part of the data available from these three credit bureaus , or none altogether. They could decide to use data that is not available from these agencies like utility and rental history. Public records, like mortgages or personal property titles, liens and deeds are often used.

Each credit scoring system uses the same set of information to determine your credit score. It assigns each component a weight , or importance. It is usually reflected as each component contributes a certain percentage towards your final credit score. Certain components, like your credit history, for instance, will have a significant impact. Other factors, such as new credit is likely to have a less impact. This is also subject to the system of scoring that is used.

Chapter 3: Why Having A Great Credit Score Is Critical

You might be wondering why all the fuss is about credit scores. The truth is that we aren't fortunate enough to be millionaires and have no liquid capital. This means we'll require any kind of loan in our lives, and often more than once.

All of us are obligated to lead. All of us require access to the basics, like electricity, water and telecom. We all require a place to reside. The credit rating of your score is one primary thing that these companies will take into consideration when they are deciding whether to offer their services.

A credit score that isn't optimal could affect you in a variety of tangible ways. The higher your credit score, the higher chances you have of receiving the services you need at the time you're looking for them, and also the less they'll cost you at the final.

Applying for an loan

There are occasions that we must take a huge, significant decision that requires financial support to make it happen. The process of getting through college is usually a matter of getting an student loan. For example, buying a car, putting up the kitchen area with new appliances or even a major event such as a wedding could require the assistance of a loan. For the majority of us buying a home without borrowing money isn't possible.

Lending institutions can look at your credit report prior to making the decision to offer you an credit or no. A low credit score (or one with a shaky credit history) appears as a high-risk customer to these lenders and can mean nothing good for you. They might agree to loan you less than you've requested, or refuse your request completely.

Interest Rates

The impact on your credit rating does not end with your being eligible for an loan or not. Even when the lender has made a decision to provide assistance, low credit score could result in a significant cost.

If your credit score falls, greater the interest rate for your loan. It is because they consider you to be an extremely risky customer. They could also offer you a longer time frame within which you can repay the loan. In the end, these two elements create a higher personal burden.

Employment Opportunites

A well-written resume and custom cover letter can help you stand apart from your competitors and allow you to get the interview. It's possible that you're impressive and charming and convince your prospective employer that you're a top applicant for this job. What you might not be aware of is the fact that credit score could be a factor and could ruin your job opportunity.

According to various studies, more than 70 percent of employers conduct Background checks for their employees. Certain employers will also examine your credit score as well. This is particularly the case for jobs that require you to manage big sums of money.

Employers are not able to check you credit reports without consent or knowledge. However, a negative financial history with a history of delayed payments or collections accounts could hurt your job chances.

Housing

Your credit score also has an impact directly on the choices for housing. The majority of landlords will require a credit score prior to letting you in as an applicant. They want to make sure that you have the funds to pay the rent and are punctual with your payment. A low credit score can result in the landlord denying your application.

There is also the purchase of an apartment or house. Most of the time, there's an amount of money to be spent that many people can't manage without borrowing. Credit agencies will check the credit scores of your clients to decide if you are able to pay for and pay off the loan or not. It will also determine the interest rate they can give you. The higher scores you have, the lower you'll end up paying.

Insurance

It's not widely known however, your credit score could impact your insurance policy too. Your credit score can impact the amount you have to have to pay for insurance premiums, whether that's auto insurance, homeowner's insurance or health insurance.

Like the banks, insurance companies are keen to determine their risk on you. When your score shows that you're not responsible when it comes to your finances this could signal that you're negligent in other areas as well.

This means you have a higher insurance risk and could impact the cost of your insurance plan. In the end, a better credit score means less risk, which means lower insurance premiums.

Chapter 4: What Is The Factor That Determines Your Credit Score

Now, you're conscious of the significance of a credit score and how it affects your financial situation. The main takeaway from now is, no whatever your circumstance having a better rating on your credit is more favorable. It can give you more options to bargain in many aspects of your financial life.

There are many different scoring systems that exist that we've had an in-depth look at a few of them. Each one of them bases their calculations on a different set data and perform calculations differently.

Credit Score is Calculated Using an algorithm

Every scoring system that is in use uses a particular formula. These formulae are private and owned by the company that developed the particular system. FICO uses its own algorithm, along with VantageScore, CE, and all other systems currently in use.

The Factors that Influence Your Credit Score

It is well-known that each credit scoring system uses various elements to calculate your score. Two systems that use the same components could produce different scores simply because they weigh these factors in different ways.

For the rest of the book, we're going to concentrate specifically on specifically the FICO scoring system in particular. It's because it is the most widely used and acceptedsystem, with more than 90% of all credit agencies using it to create its credit scores.

The information contained in this book will be as valuable in other scoring systems as well. The factors and the weighting they apply to them are going to be different. However, understanding the factors that impact your credit score, and what you can do to improve it is the same regardless of the scoring model or system that is being used.

FICO base their credit scores on information gathered from the three credit bureaus in the United States: Experian, Equifax, and TransUnion. It does not take into account other sources of information like rental or utility reports. FICO uses the credit report that is prepared by all three bureaus, and then translates the data into a three-digit score.

The algorithm used by FICO is proprietary, and therefore, not all of the details are available. However, it's publicly available knowledge that there exist five elements that affect the FICO credit rating. Each factor is weighted in accordance with importance. Take a look at the table below to get a sense of what each component is and how it will impact the final score.

Factors that influence FICO score. How Much It contributesto the FICO score to the %

Payment Histories 35

Credit Utilization 30

Credit History Length 15

New Credit 10

Credit Mix 10

What factors contribute to Your Credit Score

Five factors that affect the end FICO score. Great. But what do they actually mean? Understanding them is the first step to knowing what you can do be doing to boost your score on credit.

Payment History is responsible for 35percent of overall score, which makes it the most crucial element. FICO analyzes past behavior to predict the future's long-term behaviour.

FICO examines both the revolving loan (read credit card) as well as installment loans, that include housing and student loans, and others. FICO examines all missed payments on your loans. It examines the extent of missed payments, the frequency, and the time of missed payments.

In the words of Tommy Lee, a principal scientist at FICO A missed loan payment isn't considered to be more or less serious as a missed credit card transaction.

Credit utilization is the percentage of credit that was used to purchase. The percentage of credit utilization is 70% of your total score, it's the second-most important aspect to take into consideration.

With FICO credit utilization, it is calculated individually by credit card, as well as across many credit cards. There isn't any standard credit utilization ratio that is higher than zero that can boost your credit score.

As you can observe, these two elements together make up nearly 2/3 of the credit scores you have. It is only natural, so, when looking at ways to boost credit scores, it is best to begin with these two aspects. More on this in the future.

FICO also evaluates how long your history of credit in formulating the credit score. This adds 15% to you final score.

It's a quick calculation of the time each account has been openfor, and the amount of time from the last action for each account. FICO will consider the credit accounts of all your accounts listed here.

The amount of credit you have and makes up 10% of your final score. A new credit card will reduce your average age of the account. It can also impact your credit score if do not have many other credit-related information.

The credit mix can be considered the 5th and last element that determines the FICO score, which accounts for 10 percent of the final score. It might sound unclear, but it's actually rooted in the notion that remending various debt products will allow you to handle any kind of credit. In the case of FICO those who do not have loans or credit cards are considered to be at a higher risk than those that have credit cards or installment loans, if they've been properly managed.

The five elements listed above will give you the final score you get with FICO. VantageScore is essentially using similar criteria to FICO however, it might be weighing them differently and employs an entirely different algorithm. Other scoring systems employ these exact factors in an extent, but to a lesser degree.

Another factor that is likely to influence your credit score although it's not listed as one of FICO's top five criteria is hard inquiries. Hard inquiries occur when you apply for an loan, mortgage or credit card, and the lender or credit card issuer will check your credit score prior to making a decision. Most of the time, they require the approval of you and cannot be granted without your authorization.

How You Can Get Several Different Scores In One Go

The thing that can be confusing is that based upon the company you go to there could be multiple credit scores at the same time. There are several reasons for why this may occur.

One reason we've observed is that there are many different scoring systems that are in use. Based on the elements each system considers and the weight it assigns to them the score will definitely differ. Therefore, even if they use the same set of criteria two scoring systems such as FICO as well as VantageScore will produce different scores.

Another reason for having scores that differ is the date the scores were made. Scores are subject to change at any moment, meaning that two scores made at different times and applying the same system of scoring are likely to differ. It is possible that you take out another line credit prior to the time your previous score was obtained, or even paid off the loan. Each action reported to credit bureaus is counted.

In addition Not every lender is reported to all three credit bureaus. A handful of lenders have a report with only some or two. This implies that a credit bureau might not have all the details about you. This can either benefit or harm your score, based on the situation.

Chapter 5: Estimating Your Credit Score

It's the first thing to learn the meaning of a credit score and the best way to increase it. After you've done that, you'll want to know what your score is currently.

Since the most widely-accepted program, FICO, uses credit reports for calculating scores for your credit rating, the very first thing you must do is to obtain the credit report. It's important to note that VantageScore is also based on these credit reports, which is why it's even more important to to obtain them.

Receiving Your Free Credit Reports

The three credit bureaus in the United States, Equifax, TransUnion and Experian Each of them will provide a credit report for you. The best part is that you'll have access to all of these reports for free of cost.

It is the Fair Credit Reporting Act (FCRA) requires all three credit bureaus to provide you a report of your credit report upon your request. It is possible to request this service at least once per year.

Three credit agencies have created an online portal, toll-free number, as well as mailing addresses. You can request a complimentary annual credit score by each of them.

To order your free credit report, you can visit annualcreditreport.com or call 1-877-322-8228. It is also possible to fill out your Annual Credit Request Report Form and send it in to Annual Credit Report Request Service, P.O. Box 105281 Atlanta, GA 30348-5281.

You can request all three credit reports at one time or only one at each. Do not contact any or the credit bureaus separately. They offer annually free credit report by using the three channels mentioned above.

Important note: Beginning in 2020 and continuing through 2026, all residents of the U.S. can get 6 free credit reports every year. It is possible to do this by going to the Equifax website or by calling 1-866-349-591. This is an addition to the standard three credit reports each year that are issued by each credit bureau across the nation.

Be aware that getting your report for free requires you to give some of your personal information. You'll need to provide your name and address, as well as date of birth and Social Security number.

To ensure the security of your credit file Each credit bureau will ask for information only you be able to. This could include the total amount you pay for your car or mortgage payment. Every company can request different information since the data they collect regarding you could be derived from various sources.

If you purchase your credit report online, you will have access to them right away. If you make a purchase by telephone or postal mail, be prepared to wait for 15 days from the time the date of receipt to receive your report through the mail.

Beware of fake websites when you request free credit reports for your annual cycle. The only site legally mandated to do so is annualcreditreport.com. This official site and the three credit bureaus will ever email you emails or request you for your personal information by phone. If you do you should not provide any information since it's likely to be to be a scam.

Using Free FICO Score Estimators

The ability to take a glance at credit history is an excellent way to find out what your current financial status is. But, these reports do not give you scores.

The federal government requires credit bureaus to give you an annual credit report for free. However, there isn't a obligation to obtain FICO scores. There is a possibility that you can receive a complimentary FICO score through other subscription services but it's not an option. The only way you'll obtain it for free is when you are denied access to the product or service you want or you are offered lower-quality terms due to the FICO score. In these situations you are entitled to check what's your FICO score.

However, that doesn't mean there's nothing you can do about the situation. You can get a sense of what your FICO score is through FICO score estimation tools. Although they might not be able to give you a 100 percent accurate response, if you provide them with the correct information, they'll get close enough that they don't have any significant impact.

The FICO Score Estimator tools give you a set of multiple-choice tests based on your credit background. Instead of providing you with an accurate score, these tools make use of the information you provide them to calculate scores in a range. The questions are based on five factors that determine your FICO score which include the history of your payment, your credit utilization and length of credit history, the amount of credit you have and the credit mix.

Based on the answers you provide to the initial question You may be asked additional questions to be asked until the estimator is armed with enough information to calculate an accurate calculation.

A reasonably precise estimate with the FICO score calculator is a matter of knowing your credit background. There are many things to be aware of including what's the sum of all your outstanding loan balances, the total number of your credit applications that you've submitted recently as well as the number of credit cards you've got and the balances they carry as well as many other things.

For a fair estimate, you need to give accurate information. Since we do not have all the information in our possession it is beneficial to have the most current credit reports available. So, your projected score range is more likely to be accurate.

There are numerous websites that provide free FICO score estimation tools. However, they're all powered by myFico.com If that you enter the same information and provide the same results. Each of these sites will be able to provide what you're seeking.

* myFico.com

* bankrate.com

* whatsmyscore.org

FICO estimators are attempting to be accurate, however they're not 100% reliable. Even with the best efforts to provide precise and complete information they could fail. They might provide you with a range that is higher or lower than the actual FICO score is. The benefit, however, is that they're completely free.

If you truly need the actual FICO score you can find it at myFICO.com. You'll have to pay for it, since this is not a no-cost service. However, it will provide you with assurance that you know your exact score, without any guesswork.

It's possible to obtain your FICO score without cost however this would require the user to purchase other services or products. If you're a holder of an Discover credit card for instance your FICO score will be displayed in your statement each month. Some credit unions and banks offer the FICO score for free (and different) score to its customers. For a complete list of possible no-cost FICO score companies, go to lifelock.com as well as forbes.com.

Chapter 6: Understanding What Could Damage Your Credit Score

It might seem like a daunting task at first, however credit scores don't come from a magic wand. They are based on actual data. They are based on factual information. FICO score is based solely on your credit history that it gets from the three credit bureaus in the United States.

Knowing what a credit score means and where it comes from, how it's used, and the method of calculation, is the first step to winning. It's impossible to do when you don't know the meaning behind it and the source of it.

The other part of the battle is knowing how your financial habits could negatively impact your score on credit. Knowing the basics is well, but let's take a look at the practical side of it. We discuss common financial transactions and products and how not using them may impact your credit score.

What kind of credit do you have?

Sometimes, it's not a matter of doing something financial irresponsible that will cause you to lose points on FICO (and other scoring systems, too). It's about whether your financial habits are in line with what scoring systems consider to be "good" behavior.'

You could analyze your circumstances and conclude it's a good idea to use one credit card sufficient to cover your needs at present You're probably right. It's in its own manner it's a sound financial decision. Why would you need more credit than you actually require? The less debt you have and the less space for issues.

It's true that it could be a negative factor with your FICO score. Keep in mind that one of the factors that determine an FICO score is your credit mix. It is responsible for 10% of your total score. If you only have one credit card, or no installment loans, you are in fact affecting your score.

FICO evaluates those with multiple active, well-managed credit card and installment loans to be a less risky option than those who have just the one credit card. In other words the more credit cards you have, the more credit score.

Don't rush out to apply for a new collection of credit card as soon as you can. A large number of credit cards could be a mistake that tells bankers you're in desperate need for cash. Hard requests, which you'll need to complete when applying to credit card companies, may be a risk to you and cost you points. It's not a smooth line you need to walk and we'll explore the issue in greater detail when we discuss strategies for improving you credit scores.

Of course in the event that you don't have an active credit card or loan, you don't have a FICO score any time. It is essential to have at least one credit or loan account that's been in existence for a minimum of six months in order to be eligible for an FICO score. It's not a surprise that the credit card and loan should initially be submitted to all three credit agencies.

Credit Utilization (Amount Owed)

To recap that credit utilization is the method you utilize credit that is readily available. This section accounts for 30 percent of your overall score, therefore the way you use your credit here affects your score. This is particularly true if you own multiple credit card or multiple installment loans on your record.

One thing that can rapidly decrease your score on credit is when you max on your credit card. A card that is maxed out can reduce your score by up to 45 points. There's no set ratio to determine the amount of your balances must be in relation to the total credit limit to obtain higher scores, however less is certainly more favorable.

Another issue that can affect your credit score are errors on your credit report. Every credit institution you have a credit card and loan with is going to report to at minimum 3 credit bureaus in the United States however, mistakes can occur. False information on this page can cause you to lose points when the calculation of the credit score.

The status of an authorized account on another's credit card can affect your score. If you're added to the credit card account of someone else with the status of an authorized account you will inherit the card's payments history as well. This won't hurt your credit score in the least, but this is the reverse, provided that the owner of the credit card has handled the account well. If they've made late payments or the balance is excessive the impact will be on your credit score adversely also.

The cancellation of a credit card could affect your score on credit. Be aware that cancelling the credit card won't erase its data from your credit report immediately. A credit card account that is closed that has a high limit on credit can affect your score, particularly if you carry high-balances on other credit cards or loans. The only reason closing the credit card account will not impact the credit rating is when you don't have any balances as well as if your utilization is zero.

Consolidating debt is another factor which can affect you credit. Consolidating debt means that you combine several debt balances into a single new loan. In the long run, it will boost your credit score in the event that you make use of the account to pay off the debt off. In the short term, however, you'll notice a decrease on your credit score.

As a result, a missed payments to a credit card or loan can affect the credit score. Any single loan or card payment late by 30 days could cost someone who has an FICO score that is 780 or higher around 110 points. In reality, lenders won't declare a payment as missing to credit bureaus unless it's late by more than 60 days.

Refinancing an existing loan is in your possession can hurt your credit score a bit. It is typically because of the way in which the loan is declared. In most circumstances, the loan will not be considered new loans however, it will be the same loan but with some changes. Your score could drop a bit due to the rigorous investigation that is required to process refinancing.

In addition, making hard inquiries could affect the credit rating of your. This does not mean that you should never think about obtaining an additional loans or credit cards. If five or more prospective mortgage lenders look over their credit history within the next 30 days of searching to find the best deal It's only one credit inquiry, also called a "hard pull.' The one inquiry is likely to cost you approximately five points. The effect isn't too large, considering that it will only impact the credit rating for a single year.

Payment History

Looking at how you can use the FICO score system we found that the history of your payments contributes the highest amount on your rating. At 35%, it's the biggest effect on credit scores, and especially in the long run.

Since history is something you build over time, each step you take in the context of managing your credit cards and loans will be reflected in this score. The better managed the credit cards you have are more successful your score will be.

One of the main factors that can impact your score when you review payments history is the absence of loans and card payments. We've already seen that one missed payment could lower your score up to 110 points. It's not difficult to see that multiple failed payments can cause serious harm to the credit rating. In fact, a missed payment could remain at the top of your credit score for as long as seven years. This is a long time to make a payment for a minor error.

Also, be aware of the credit card you are authorized signatory of since you will inherit the account's history of payments. If the card's primary owner has a great credit history that is good, it will reflect positively in your score, too. But the reverse is valid. If your card has negative or score-killing history and your score is also affected, it will be affected.

The errors on your credit report impact not just the score of your credit utilization, but also your credit history. Every mistake you make in your credit file is there until it is corrected. As time passes, the errors become more frequent, resulting in the loss of valuable credit score points.

If you file for bankruptcy at any point you will experience huge effect on the credit rating of yours, which can drop it from 130 to the 240th percentile. The bankruptcy will remain in your credit file for as long as 10 years.

The foreclosure process is another one which can severely damage the credit rating of your. When it is on your credit report over a period of seven years, it could cause you to lose up to 160 points. A foreclosure occurs when your mortgage lender seizes the property mortgaged due to inability to pay back the loan.

Deeds in lieu are a procedure which allows homeowners to transfer the home to the mortgage lender in order to stay out of foreclosure. The lender may then decide to sell the property to pay for its loss. This could lower your credit score by up to 120 points. This is extremely low but is still better than foreclosure. There is a chance of further negative effects in your score due to not paying mortgage payments, but.

Sometimes, a property which is considered to be underwater cannot be sold for an amount that is sufficient to pay off the loan for the mortgage. A short sale happens when the mortgage company accepts an amount that is less than the balance of the original loan. It could also affect your credit score severely by costing as high as 150 points.

The cost of collection and charge-offs is also you points on your credit card. A charge-off occurs the process whereby a creditor eliminates an unpaid debt off its books. It usually happens when the debt is more than 180 days over the due date. The term "collection" refers to the process whereby a creditor offers the unpaid debt to a third party , or engages an outside company to collect the debt for them.

A single charge can lower an excellent credit score of more than 700 points by up to 100 points. Collections stay visible on the credit reports for as long as seven years. The more recent your collection account is, the more detrimental it is to your score on credit. It is the FICO 8 rating system does not take into account collections with a balance that is less than $100.

Another option if you're in a bind is to settle your debt. The process of settling the debt with a creditor at a lower amount than the originally due will affect your credit score, too. You could be able to lose anywhere from 45 points to 100 points in this.

The duration of the credit history

The duration of credit histories is crucial in determining the FICO score. As we have already mentioned anyone who has not used a credit card or had a loan taken out is not eligible for a FICO score because they don't have a credit background to calculate the score on.

In summary, you must to have an open credit card or loan account that was open and active for at least six months in order to earn FICO scores. The lending institution you used to get the loan has prepared an assessment of your credit activity in this period and this is enough to allow FICO to provide you with an assessment.

Credit history is not about one particular thing you do or don't do. It's about having a good overall credit history that is free of defaulted payment, debt settlements, and the rest of the things which can affect your credit score. If you have well-managed loans and credit card payments A longer track record is superior to a shorter one. It shows potential creditors that you're trustworthy for a long period of time.

Similar to the other aspects you should be aware of when looking at your credit use and payments could also be an important factor. What number and type of loans do you have as well as the amount of credit cards you've got and the manner in which you've utilized them, as well as whether you've paid off all of your outstanding debts in date or not. All of these are reflected in your credit history. The majority of the negative items will remain on your credit report for at least two years, occasionally, as long as 10.

A prospective creditor who you've applied for will always have an examination of your credit score prior to making a decision. A strong credit history is a good sign, proving to your potential lender that you know how to manage your finances and are accountable in the use of money. The reverse is relevant. A lengthy credit history that is replete of missed payments, collections and chargeoffs will certainly affect your credit score, and will cause a lender to be less likely to lend you their services.

Chapter 7: Tips To Enhance Your Credit Score

As of now, I'm hoping you've got a clear understanding of the things your credit score is in the first place, and, most important, what could harm it. Understanding the factors that affect your credit score will give you the decision of the steps you can take to improve it significantly.

You've probably also spent the time to request your free credit report that are from each of the three credit bureaus in the United States. If you haven't yet, please take the time to do so via annualcreditreport.com. It's not expensive and you'll receive your reports right away.

If you've received your credit reports then you're viewing a fairly accurate estimation of the range your FICO score falls within. For a quick reminder there are plenty of sites that offer this for you at no cost, however they all run on myFICO.com. If you want to know your actual FICO score it is possible to obtain it from this site, but for a fee.

It's a bit daunting to take a look at the credit score you have about you and your credit score, but you'll have to confront in the near future or sooner. Knowing your credit score isn't as good is a lot more damaging than knowing that you have a low one. It is better to be to the bull's horns, and face up to the reality. After you've made the leap and calculate your score then you can begin taking immediately steps to improve it.

If you're FICO score estimator informed you that your score was in the top range, then congratulations. It means you have a flawless credit record and have been exceptionally responsible with managing your money. You probably already employ some of the techniques we'll discuss below, but you could be able to come away with some new concepts.

If you have scores that are good or very excellent the chances are you're doing fairly well you can likely increase your score up to an outstanding level pretty quickly. Certain of the techniques are ones you've already been practicing while others might be completely brand new for you. Be sure to pay focus on this section and executing using these suggestions will bring your score to an excellent level quickly.

If your score is judged to be poor or fair There's no way to go to go about it. It is imperative to take action to improve your score and you must perform it quickly. The strategies listed below, more than one time is a good idea, to give you an ideal start.

Making improvements to your credit score can be quite simple and easy. It's all you need is to take some time to figure out the reasons that led to your score being to be so low in the initial place (which most likely you've already completed in the past). Once you've figured this out established, you'll know what went wrong and the reason. It's easy to devise a strategy to improve your score by using the strategies that we'll explain below. A lot of the things we'll talk about is achievable in a matter of minutes, so you'll begin to see your score rise immediately.

Review and Disput Your Credit Reports

The first step in increasing your score on credit is to get access to and looking over your credit reports. You're entitled to one FREE credit file from the three credit bureaus in the United States (Equifax, TransUnion, and

Experian) each year for a period of 12 months. You can request these three reports at once or request them separately. The request for your credit report does not affect your credit score in any way.

After you have your report You will have a clearer idea of what's actually documented in your financial records. This is the place to determine what is working for you, and what's not.

The first thing you should start to look for is mistakes. The individuals who input the information into these reports aren't 100% accurate, and mistakes could be made and they do happen. In the United States, FCRA (Fair credit reporting act) provides you with the right to a complete credit report. You are able to challenge any errors that you spot within your credit reports, by notifying the credit bureau that you are concerned about who will then look into the matter within 30 days.

Birthdays, addresses and addresses frequently suffer from mistakes. Social security numbers can be interchangeable, and the payment date could be entered incorrectly.

Finding an error on your credit report corrected could have immediate and visible outcomes. For instance, if already have a history late payments , and someone enters an actual payment that you paid on time but is deemed to be late, it can affect your credit score very significantly.

Do not delay, and report any errors you discover immediately. If you are quick to notify the credit bureau, the quicker it can be fixed and improve the credit rating of yours.

While at the same time be sure to report information as false only if you truly believe it is. Falsifying documents, or giving incorrect information could see you in trouble. You aren't making yourself any good impression by attempting to deceive yourself. It won't alter your score but you'll be creating a negative image in the eyes of credit agencies.

In the event of reporting mistakes Many financial experts suggest filing it in writing rather than online. When you file your dispute using the hard copy postal mail and certified creates an evidence trail and accountability. This doesn't allow the credit company to avoid certain actions including giving you an official response in writing and sending your details for your lenders.

It is also crucial to refer your complaint to the correct organization. This is usually the credit agency , not your creditor.

Another thing to be on the lookout for is fraud. If you review your credit reports and discover the credit request you didn't make you should immediately report it. It's not just affecting your score on credit, but it also could mean that your financial security is in danger.

Examine your credit reports each year Then go over them using a fine-toothed comb to look for any mistakes. Any errors you find should be reported promptly. Fixing those mistakes is the most efficient method of improving the credit rating of your.

Control Your Bill Payments and Get Your Bills Under Kontrolle

To be truthful, the primary reason why most people who have poor credit scores is that it is because their credit record isn't good. Every credit card or credit account that you are applying for gets into your credit file, as are your transactions.

Beware of late payments at all cost. This is the short and long of it. We're all very busy and often have to be in ten places at time, making it easy to miss when your next the payment due. There are methods to handle your payment, however.

You can make a simple filing system that keeps the track of your bills for the month. The filing system could be paper or on digital. There are a lot of easy-to-use, free applications for phones and desktops that are designed to help you keep track of your accounts. You can also create due-date reminders on your phone calendar to make sure you don't overlook an invoice that's due.

Another option is to automate the payment of bills directly from the bank account. Based on the banker you use the cost of this service might cost you just a little. However, in the end, paying this cost is much less than having a low credit score because of late or missed payments.

Another option to think about is to pay the entire, or as many of your monthly bills to one credit card. This way it is important to be sure to make the balance payment each month in full in order to avoid interest fees. This will help you simplify the bill payment process, since it only requires only one major payment each month, as opposed to many smaller ones.

If you fail to make the payment, you should contact your creditor right away to establish an arrangement for payment. It will lessen negative impact to your credit rating.

Repairing your credit history isn't an instant process and requires time. Remember that this one aspect makes up 35 percent of your credit score. In time, a record of regularly scheduled, timely payments will lead to an improvement on you FICO score.

Limit Your Credit Utilization

The amount of credit you use is 2nd most important factor that affects your FICO score, after the payment history. It is responsible for 30% of you final rating. Simply put, it's the amount of your credit limit that you are making use of at any given moment.

The best method of managing the amount of credit you use is to settle all of your outstanding balances every month. It's not always as easy and you may not be able to accomplish this immediately. An ideal place to start is to focus on keeping your balance to 30 percent of your credit limit. After that, you could slowly work to reduce your balance down until it is 10%, or less than the limit of your credit. A 10% limit is the best to boost the credit rating of your.

One of the best ways to avoid over-using your limit on credit is to utilize an alert for high balances that comes with those credit cards. This way, you will be able to put off adding additional charges to your credit card in the event that the ratio of credit utilization is increasing.

If you are confident that you will not give in to the urge to spend more money then you may also approach your credit card company to raise your credit limit. This will increase the ratio of your credit utilization, as long as your balance doesn't rise simultaneously. In turn, this will increase your credit score quickly. Requesting an increase in credit limits is a simple process for all credit card businesses. It is usually possible to request it via the internet or by phone.

Limit your requests/inquiries to New Credit

A number of times when discussing how to improve the credit rating of yours, we've also talked about what's known as hard inquiries. There are two kinds of credit inquiries: hard and soft.

Soft inquiries can involve the checking of your credit score or giving a prospective employer permission to look into your credit. Financial institutions that conduct checks that you have already done business can also be considered soft inquiries. For instance the credit card company with whom you have a relationship might need to look over your account to determine if they're planning to offer you pre-approved credit deals.

Soft inquiries don't affect the credit rating in any manner and you shouldn't worry about it.

Hard inquiries However, hard inquiries will count against the credit score. They can negatively affect the score for up to two years. Hard inquiries can occur at whenever you apply for credit. The loan could comprise a car loan, a new credit card or different type of loan.

A number of credit inquiries to different institutions about the same loan can count as one single inquiry, as long as they are made over a period of 30 days. For instance, you could request information from five or four lenders while searching to find the most lucrative mortgage loan.

However, applying for credit cards, car loan or mortgage loans within a short amount of time of each other is a completely different situation. Each of these is considered as a distinct hard inquiry since they're completely distinct, and it is sure to harm the credit rating of your. Some lenders may interpret this to mean you're in financial trouble or have exceeded your financial capability and consider you to be an increased risk.

If you're working at improving your credit score score, do not apply for new credit for a few months, or, if you have to limit yourself to a certain amount. There are a few situations where applying for an additional line of credit might assist, but we'll get into this in the future.

Be aware when using credit Cards

Credit cards are a useful tool however, you must be aware of how to use them. When you purchase credit card, overspending and then maxing out your credit limit will lead you to nowhere.

This has been discussed in the past, but it's worth repeating. Keep your credit card balances low. One good guideline is to limit your credit to 30 percent of your credit limit. This will help to avoid issues in the form of creditors and poor credit scores.

The credit utilization portion that makes up your FICO score measures the ratio of your credit utilization. Although there's no exact number for this but 10% of your total debt is a good figure to target towards. Don't let your ratio of credit utilization rise above 10% and your credit score will improve for it.

If you're unable to get the credit utilization ratio to the levels you desire then you may decide to create a new line credit. So long as it's only one line of credit and not many in a row, the invasive inquiry you make during the process won't affect your score significantly.

However, the new credit card will increase your limit on credit, which improves the ratio of your credit utilization (and thus you score). So long as your balance does not increase in the same way you'll have improved to improve your FICO score.

Keep in mind that 10 percent or more of your FICO score is derived from credit card purchases. By judiciously introducing an additional credit card will benefit you, not against you.

The length of your credit history, a different element in the FICO score, considers the length of time you've been using the credit card you've been using. A credit score that is older is thought to be more attractive and can appeal more to lenders. If your credit history is solid and has a long credit history, subsequent credit applications are more likely to be accepted.

If you have any old loans with an excellent history of on-time payments, like an account for student loans Don't be rushed to close the accounts. They'll add to your credit score due to the fact that they're not in delinquency.

Also, if you own older credit cards that you don't use do not be eager to close the accounts. Closing a credit line when you're carrying an outstanding balance on another credit card will decrease your credit available and increasing the ratio of your credit utilization. The closing of one credit card will reduce a few points from your score.

If you are forced to end a credit line, possibly because of annual or monthly charges and you have a balance of more than to zero by first paying off each balance on each card you have. This will let you stop using the card, without affecting the ratio of your credit utilization and thus improving your score on credit.

Learn Which Debts You Should Pay Off First

If you have delinquent accounts or collection accounts charge-offs, you should take the time to settle these issues. For instance, if you have a credit card that has multiple missed or late payments, do not get caught by stressing over the amount due. Instead, devise an action plan to make every payment on time and without failure. Making this plan won't erase your bad past however it will make your credit history from that point to.

When we talk about getting rid of debt Don't make a bankruptcy declaration in an effort to escape an economic crisis. It might be attractive, but this can severely impact your score on credit. The worst part is the fact that this information can stay the credit reports for as long as 10 years, which makes new credit extremely difficult to obtain. This is not the cost you'd like to be paying.

If you're dealing with collection accounts or charge-offs, you'll need to choose which option makes more sense, either paying the accounts to the full amount or offering your creditor a payment. In the event of clearing collections and charge-offs may improve your credit score tiny. This is because the more recent FICO as well as VantageScore models do not have negative effects to the collections that have been paid off.

Be careful when paying off debts that are old. If a debt is not paid within 180 days of the due date will typically be billed to the debtor. This means that they don't have to make any further payment on the debt. Making payments on a charge-off account will reactivate the debt which can lower the credit rating. In this regard, you must be wary whenever dealing with collections agencies. They are very effective in threatening you to pay the credit. Make sure you check everything and require a written proof.

Make use of a "Thin Financial File' your advantage

A weak credit score indicates that you do not have the credit history needed to get an FICO (or another) score on your credit. This is a problem when you eventually require an credit line. However, don't fret there are options to improve your credit score and get yourself a great score.

UltraFICO is one of the ways you can improve your credit score even if it's been a while since you took out a loan, or had credit cards. The program is completely free and relies on your banking information to calculate your FICO score. It is important to pay your bills on time with the bank, staying away from overdrafts and keeping savings are a few factors that could help in improving your score. Also, maintaining an account with a bank for more time.

Similar programs include ExperianBoost. It records financial information that aren't typically included in your credit report. Additionally, it also includes bank history and utility payments. The program is accessible for free and created to aid people who are good at paying their bills in time.

Another option is for those who rent their houses. If you pay rent on a monthly basis There are a variety of services that offer credit when making timely payments. Rent Track and Rental Kharma are two well-known ones which report directly to credit bureaus on behalf of you. Be aware that the credit you earn from renting can only impact your VantageScore but not your FICO score.

Utilize Monitoring Services for Credit Monitoring Services

The various strategies we've spoken about in the past will be a big help to improve your score on credit. Certain strategies, such as reporting mistakes in your credit report will begin to take effect immediately. Other things, such as the better management of your payment or credit use, could take longer.

Once you've decided which strategies are effective for you and what you have to accomplish, it's a good to be aware of the way your credit score is altering as time passes. This is the point where credit monitoring services come into.

These services perform exactly as the name implies that they look for any changes to the credit score of yours, like opening a new credit card and an existing one has been paid for. They usually also grant you access to at minimum an account of one of your scores on each of the three bureaus in the national system, which are regularly updated.

A lot applications are completely free to use and assist you in keeping your finances in order. They also serve as a great method to avoid identity theft and fraud. For instance, if you get an alert that an account with a new credit card is being recorded in your file, but was not opened the account, immediately call the credit card company you use and notify them of any the suspected fraud.

The Bottom Line

In the final analysis, having a great credit score is crucial. In the near future you'll need to make an crucial decision in your life which will require you to use any kind of credit. It could be to continue your education, purchase cars or homes or renovating your kitchen.

While there are many easy ways to boost the credit rating of your business, you'll experience more and better results following sound strategies for managing your finances like keeping a clean credit history and using it in a reasonable way. The results could take months or even weeks to show up and you'll be delighted when they show up.

Chapter 8: How Does My Score Influences My Score?

Six factors are the most influential on your credit score, so it's your responsibility to pay attention to all of them if are hoping to maintain a score that is as close as 850.

Credit card usage The credit card utilization rate is the percentage of credit you have available in relation to the amount you're making use of at moment. It is determined by simply dividing the credit card balances by the total limit of all your cards. Therefore, it's recommended to consider applying for several credit cards even if you do not plan on using them. It is essential to remember that this figure is not determined based on the amount of any card, which means that you don't need to think about keeping an account balance or the possibility of rolling it over each month. It's always a good decision to pay the credit card charges at the close of the month rather than.

In time payments: Paying your bills punctually is among the most effective ways to ensure that you have a good credit score. It's a huge factor in influencing your credit score, so when you fail to make some payments, your score is most likely to be impacted because of it.

Derogatory marks: The negative mark on credit report include banksruptcies, foreclosures, liens and accounts in collections. All of them will impact your credit score in a significant way as foreclosures and bankruptcies being the most severe. The derogatory marks can remain on your file for up to 10 years. If they're accurate they are not something you can do to get rid of them before they are too late. The most common amount the derogatory mark can reduce the credit of yours is 50 points.

The amount of money you pay to get towards the derogatory marking does not have any bearing on your credit score. This means that even just one dollar transferred to collections can affect your credit score by 50 points. The date on which you received the derogatory mark can be a factor however, and is determined by when the negative event took place and not the date it took place. For instance, if you were in default on a loan in 2012, but the account wasn't referred into collections till 2017,, it will be classified as a derogatory mark that was made in the past and the seven-year window begins in 2017 not 2012. It is also important to be aware the fact that the mark is going to remain on your file regardless the fact that you've in the past paid off the collection or lien.

Line of credit age age of your credit lines is simply a measure of the length of time you've been building credit. Creditors want to see you have a history of managing credit successfully, as it helps them decide if you're an investment that is risky or not. The longer your credit historyis, the more likely that you've been able to manage your credit successfully. Therefore, it's not recommended to close the old accounts on credit cards even if you do not make use of them anymore. This will not only reduce your overall available credit, but it can decrease your credit line's age average too. This isn't limited to credit cards, but also personal loans as well as student loans, mortgages, and auto loans too.

The number of accounts In general the more credit lines that you own, the better the credit rating will get because it indicates that you've received credit from many lenders. It is recommended to be able to have an assortment of revolving and installment lines to get the most benefit. But that doesn't mean you'll be rushing out to open as many credit card accounts as possible, however, since this aspect is less important on your score than the majority of.

Amount of hard credit inquiries When a creditor examines your credit score for items like mortgages credit card, business or personal loan such as a student loan and auto loans, they could impact the credit rating by few percentage points. The effect usually fades after a couple of months, as it is not made an habit of advertising these kinds of checks. The effect is cumulative but having several inquiries about hard credit in an extremely short time isn't recommended.

FICO Scoring Model FICO Scoring Model

You've heard"FICO" or FICO when talking about credit scores. It is among the most popular ways of scoring credit that is performed through Fair Issacs Corporation or FICO. If a lender wants to lend you money, they'll be looking to see the FICO score is as well as a few other items that are listed in your credit report to ensure that they know the level of risk in lending you money , and whether they should lend credit, or not. There are many elements to consider before when the FICO score is determined. A few of them are the types of credit you use, your history of payments, the number of credit accounts, length of credit history as well as your current state of debt.

Presently, FICO is basically an analytics software firm. The company's name used to be Fair Issacs Corporation, but the name was changed in 2009. The credit scores this company produces are those that are most commonly used. If you contact an institution for the purpose of borrowing money, they'll make use of these scores to determine whether they will lend you money or not.

The scores typically range between 300 to 800. You'll be able to tell if your credit score is excellent in the event that your score is greater than 600, however when it's less than 620, the borrowing process will be difficult. When compared with other scoring models FICO scores are the ones most commonly employed. If you go to the mortgage industry it will be apparent that a lot of people adhere to strict rules regarding having a minimum FICO score to receive approval. This is why many people give FICO the most focus and strive to keep their FICO score over all other scores.

I'm sure you've been told numerous times that your FICO score must be something like this or that and then only you receive the credit that you're looking for. Therefore, this score increases its importance among common people. But , not everyone knows the significance of it and it's significance is. Because this score is so significant it is becoming more important that people need to know what it means rather than simply following what is happening or accepting it is important. FICO score is significant.

How do you calculate FICO Scores?

If you think anyone could know how FICO score is calculated, then the truth is that it's not in this way. The company is keeping the formula secret, and they don't release any information about exactly how the scores are determined. It's basically an ingenuous formula. Additionally, the scores aren't created from the corporation. The software is developed by the company. The identical software is used for TransUnion, Experian, and Equifax the main credit bureaus. The formula used by FICO is utilized across all the bureaus and they input their information into the formula to get the results. However, there is a difference in all this, and that is that an outline of the formula is provided by FICO to let consumers be aware of which agencies are considered to be weighted and utilized and we will examine them in this article -

The history of your payments is whether you've been paying your credit on time or not. Every line of credit will be listed in your credit report and if you've been late in paying them, this will also be reported. For example, if were able to pay the debt 30 or 60 days or more than 120 days after the due date, this will be mentioned in your credit report. This is 35% of your total score.

Accounts Owed - Being in outstanding debt is not positive, and this is something we can all most likely agree on. It all comes down to the amount you are obligated to pay to somebody. On the other hand you must understand that your credit score will not instantly fall because you are in debt. What's important is the proportion of amounts of credit that are available and due. For instance

If a person is owed $20000, and at the same time the credit cards have exceeded their maximum limit for drawing and all credit cards have been fully extended, the credit score for that person is likely to be lower than those who have a debt of $80000 , but none of his accounts exceeded the limit. This is 30percent of overall score.

Credit Mix - Like its title suggests, it evaluates the various accounts a person holds. If you'd like your credit score to appear a good one the range of accounts should be solid, such as credit cards, mortgages and various retail accounts and car loans. It will make up 10% of your score.

Credit History Length: In general your credit score will be automatically excellent in the event that you have a credit history that is lengthy. However, this is not the case in specific situations. If the circumstances are in your favor of you, then you will achieve a great score with a credit score that isn't long. This is 15% of your score.

A New Credit Card if there are any accounts which were recently opened, it is often referred to as "new credit. If you've opened multiple accounts in an amount of time which is a bit small, your score will be automatically diminished due to the risk of risk associated with. This is 10% of your total score.

The Complete Guide to the Different Versions of FICO

The calculations for the FICO are constantly updated since it was created this is the reason why the firm releases updated versions regularly. The original variant of FICO score calculator was introduced in 1989. If a newer version comes out, lenders have the option of using the calculation at their discretion. Furthermore, whether an institution wants to upgrade to the most recent version , or even not their decision and, as such there is no obligation to do so.

Version 8 or FICO 8 was launched in 2009. One of the great features of FICO 8 is the fact that it is reliable because of the distinctive features added to the algorithm that calculates the score base.

The primary purpose behind the FICO score is the same for all versions. Its purpose is to demonstrate to the borrower that they are required to pay their debts and behave in a manner that is responsible. If you've been paying your debts and loan EMIs punctually, your scores will be automatically very high. It is also important to keep your balances on credit cards at a minimum and don't create new accounts until you have an item in mind for purchase. If, on the other hand, you have a history of frequent delinquencies, you will likely suffer from lower credit scores. This means that you shouldn't make rash credit decision you make. The FICO 8 did not take note of the collection accounts completely where there was a minimum balance of just $100 that was not in place.

Credit cards that are highly utilized received a higher level of sensitivity when calculating FICO 8 rating. In simple words, if you're an borrowers, the score of your credit card will get negatively affected if you have active credit cards have very low balances. If you compare it to earlier versions of FICO which were based on late payments, all late payments were dealt with as if made after good judgement. If your late payment is an isolated incident and your overall finances are in good order, your score won't be affected by the late payment. In addition, to represent the risk in a more effective manner that is more precise statistically There are more types of people within FICO 8. This was mostly due to the fact that the previous system was that those with good credit histories were deemed to be by the same criteria as those who had none. However, this change separated the two categories.

In the year 2016 FICO score 9 was made public and it has some minor modifications to the information in score 8 with regard to the sensitivity of rental histories and medical collection accounts and also , it's now looked upon with a smile when you have a third third-party collection that is completely paid. To date, however, FICO 9 score has not yet been implemented at one of the credit agencies that are major.

Industry-specific FICO Scores

Sometimes, FICO scores are adjusted to make them ideal for products belonging to a particular sector. One example is auto loans and credit cards. The basic Fico score models and the specific to the industry FICO scores are built on the same basis, but because every industry comes with its own risk, this is why the scores were designed to correspond with the industry's risk. The most important advantage is that the people who lend funds have up-to-date information in their possession. This allows them to make the right decisions to ensure that the borrowers get the best credit.

The probability of a person borrowing not repaying the loan in full later on as is the normal way to go as measured using the base FICO score. It could be an unsecured student credit card, loan or even mortgage. In the case of the industry FICO scores, it has the characteristics of the basic scores, however, in addition to that it also conducts a more refined risk assessment for that specific sector and is specifically tailored to each kind of credit. For instance the FICO Bankcard Score can be used to evaluate credit cards while the FICO Auto Score can be used intended for auto lenders.

Many people are confused about which type of FICO score they should be looking at and this is why I've put together a simple guide to help those of you.

If you're looking to purchase a vehicle using finance and you are looking to finance it, FICO Auto Scores are what you're going to require. If you are looking to evaluate your credit they will give you the advantage.

In the same way, if you're planning make an application for a credit card, it's not just the FICO Score which will be utilized by the lender, but as well your FICO Score for your bank card.

For credit scores for mortgages the version of FICO scores that existed prior to version 8.8 are those most commonly utilized. You ought to be aware of them too.

The basic FICO Score of 8 will be the one most often used in situations such as student loans, and personal loans.

Another question that many people ask is closing their credit will aid in improving your FICO Score 8, however this won't assist since a closed credit card will not be included as a factor in an FICO score. However, if the account that was closed was associated with any missed payments, even if they were previously, the account could be weighed as a factor against your score.

Additionally, you must be aware that, even though it's more popular than the FICO score which is most frequently used, there's another score table increasing in popularity. It is known as the Vantage Score. About 10% of businesses are currently using the Vantage Score. The method of calculating Vantage Score is very different from FICO. For Vantage Score the payment history is comprised 40 percent of the score. credit-related accounts that are used with 20% each, different types of credit and old account for 21 percent, recent inquiries or behavior is 5% of the score, your available account for credit at 3% and the total amount of debt or balance accounts for 11 percent.

The Difference Between FICO and Other Credit Scores

Another concern you could ask yourself is the difference among and the FICO score and the other credit scores. Some are available. For starters with these scores, they are the only ones developed through Fair Isaac Corporation. Fair Isaac Corporation and they are utilized by around 90% of the most reputable lenders when it comes to making lending decisions in general.

The reason behind this is because FICO scores will be viewed as the standard for making accurate and fair judgements about the creditworthiness and creditworthiness of an individual. They've been able to assist millions of people gain the credit they require to fulfill a variety of needs.

There are other credit scores that are available that are able to be utilized in certain circumstances. They are going determine the amount they provide you with in a different way as the FICO score could. While it might appear as if some of the other scores are like the ones we can see in FICO scores, they are not. FICO scores, they aren't. Only FICO scores will be used by the majority among the best lenders that you would like to take out a loan from, and although other scores are useful for monitoring your score if you'd like, the most effective option is to use your FICO score.

What is a Credit Report?

Credit reports are a summary of the complete history of your financial obligations.

It also provides a summary of the balances you owe on any credit line or debit that you are carrying in the present.

When you use the social security number (SSN) to obtain money or to establish credit lines it is reported by your credit score.

In the same way, when you make payments on your credit card or loan the transaction is noted in your credit file.

If you've got any negative credit-related items including bankruptcy, liens, collections and foreclosures, they will be listed in your credit score.

In addition, credit reports contain recent inquiries about credit, along with the name and address verification details.

Understanding Credit Report

There are many various categories that are included on the report, which requires you take a look at various aspects to ensure you have a credit rating that is good enough to allow you to obtain what you want.

The most desirable scores are those with above 900, but few individuals can attain this. If you score greater than 700, you've got good credit and you're almost assured of any credit you may seek. But keep in mind that various kinds of credit card firms or agencies will require an entirely different score.

If you score around 600, you stand an excellent chance of getting credit at most places, however, not every. However, this isn't a guarantee. There are a lot of organizations that are willing to take as a small risk.

The credit score you have is an indicator of how big a chance it will be to grant credit. When you first begin applying for credit, you'll have an unsatisfactory credit score. The person who is checking your score that there's the risk of high that is involved. This is the reason your score is not high. When you make more recorded payments, your score will go up as the probability of not being able to pay for something is decreasing.

It's not only missed or late payments that affect you with regard in your score on credit.

Let's dissect them a bit and then look over what's on your credit reports.

The worst thing that you can get, such as judgments or tax liens against you. All of them will leave a huge dent in your credit score. They will be working to your disadvantage for a long period of time (up to seven years). Don't take these on in the least, if you are able to avoid it.

The next step is to look at the credit items you have. This includes loans, credit cards mortgages, and any other credit card you've used previously. A majority of accounts that are older (closed longer than 10 years in the past) aren't reported unless there was a collection made against the account.

Every timely payment will be counted to your benefit, while every late payment collection, missed payment, or late payment will be counted against you. Each balance is recorded in addition to high balances, and they are also counted against you.

We've mentioned before that you should have a good credit balance However, you should also aim to keep a low amount of credit that you're using. What the credit report agency does is analyze the amount you're able to spend on all your credit cards, and then take that number and add it up. This is your credit balance. Then they'll examine how much you have to pay on those cards and add them total.

The balance owed can be divided in half by the total available, and this is the total percentage of your balance. You should reduce this percentage as it will reflect well to your credit report. A higher percentage could appear bad and reduce your credit score.

The total number of accounts you have and the kinds of accounts you have will be reflected in your score. It is recommended to have a decent amount of account (more than 10) in order to ensure that you are able to keep them all up-to-date.

The number of inquiries you make will impact your score. You should reduce the number of inquiries you make since everyone can be a minor negative impact on your credit score. The reason for this is that they occur every time you request credit. This is why you should apply for credit less frequently and only when you're confident that you'll be granted it. The credit you receive will increase your credit score more than it would hurt the inquiry.

You should be aware of these important points with regard to your credit score:

Have multiple Accounts (10 or more)?

* Ensure that all accounts are current.

* Stay clear of public records.

* Keep your available balance high

* Make sure to keep the balance in use at a low level.

* Do not request credit unless you absolutely need to

Don't request credit for a loan unless confident you'll get accepted

* Disput accounts that aren't accurate

* Pay off any accounts that are past due and pay off collection accounts

If you do all these actions, the credit rating will improve in time. It'll take time and you'll need to be persistent however, you'll be able to raise the credit rating back to normal. When you've managed to get your score up you'll discover it's more easy to eliminate the debt, and will begin saving more effectively and saving more.

The reason why your credit score is a factor is that your credit score will have an impact on the approval you receive to get everything you need from credit card, car loans to mortgages. It is also a factor in the interest rates you're offered. In the end, if you're debt free, that you'll have more money save for your savings. It's a win all the way around.

What is A Credit History?

A credit report is compiled by utilizing data provided by banks, financial institutions, as well as electric, telephone or insurance businesses. This is the one that allows you to be granted credit.

What can I do to get my Credit History?

Begin by acquiring the cell phone plan, department store card or cable television. Additionally, you can get an installment loan from your trusted financial institution. A financial product, such as the savings account is an option for getting credit history.

What is a Credit Rating?

It is a rating assigned by measurement agencies to credit or debts of various businesses, governments, or individuals in accordance with their credit score. It is determined by the credit background of a legal or natural person , and more importantly the ability to repay the money. The capacity is determined by the analysis of all assets and liabilities of the subject being assessed. Credit ratings vary from 300-850. A low score indicates less creditworthiness while a higher rating indicates greater creditworthiness.

This is how you ruin Your Credit History

Then you start to get an unflattering track record for having trouble paying credit card debts in time. Another option is to not pay one who was your bank's guarantor and failed to pay the bill in time. How many family members and friends acted as guarantors to their acquaintances to pay for the loan, and at the end of the day it was they that had to settle a debt that wasn't their own due to the fact that the person could not pay the outstanding bill.

In the same way, not having enough the time required to pay back an outstanding loan will affect your credit report. There is no reason for this, because the automatic debits on cards are paid for by you and, naturally, if you have this option enabled in your system. If you're on some kind of service, such as or a cellphone plan, and you don't make the payment or do it wrong and you don't pay, you erase your past. You were required to pay to pay for the Internet service that they provide you, but you didn't pay could be a reason to sue you.

How many days of late Payments Am I Allowed? What Effect Does It Have On My Credit Score?

If you've never been in a day of late payment that's your credit score. This means you're likely to be a good candidate for a loan according to banks. If, despite all your payments and other obligations, you do not have this score it could be because you were not more than six months behind. After six months, when you've gotten caught up on your account, you could be able to qualify as normal.

Clients with potential issues. You can be considered a qualified client when you're between 9 and 30 days behind. The installment is only due and make your regular payments in the months following until you reach the normal level of qualification. If you have this credit you are still able to apply to personal loans but not for huge amounts of money. Additionally, your interest rate may be slightly higher.

Deficient customer. If you fall into this category, it must be longer than 30 days, and not more than 60-day of delay. You won't be able to obtain fresh loans at any banks.

Doubtful Client. If your payment has been late for more than 60 days or less than 120 days. Your credit is not sufficient to make interest payments.

Client who is bankrupt. The time to repay your debt is greater than 120 days. You've stopped paying your debts. Be prepared, it's the lowest credit score. Banks consider it likely that you won't be able to repay therefore the possibility of a loan seems unlikely.

Another way to destroy your credit score is to make use of your credit card to get supposed rebates (which will eventually disappear) and not to consider budgets when you apply for credit to finance an important occasion (such as your wedding or travel).

Be wary of creditors who propose to "Reduce" or "Skip" payments. It's better to refinance

A small amount of money while it may seem better than never paying but it's a tiny danger. Since, even if pay the minimum amount in order that your account remains active and doesn't generate interest, it's an opportunity to result in that balance of your credit card to increase until it's almost inaccessible.

If you are considering refinancing your debt, work with your bank to change the date of your credit payments for the next six months. If you're in debt on your payment regardless of whether it's for one month, the best alternative is the refinancing option. The issue in applying for this option can be the fact that your credit scores could alter and stay in that state for the next six months.

Think about the possibility of a debt consolidation credit card or balance transfer to a credit card with lower interest. It's about making your monthly payment into a single installment, leading to lower monthly payments. This is targeted at those who have a credit card debt that typically is characterized by higher rates of interest. If you own a house or other property of value which you can utilize to secure the loan, then you could risk losing it if you are unable to pay back the loan.

You can save money. You could be able to pay off debts faster. For instance having a full-time job more consulting (in which you can develop your expertise and offer specific services) as well as additional payment for overtime and bonuses can be a great foundation for the things you want to buy even if you do it small by little. But you can, you can.

There are many ways to save money. Some of them are striking is kakeibo. It's an ancient Japanese savings strategy that involves using notebooks. It tracks at the start of each month, your income and fixed expenses like rent or mortgage electric, self-assessment, and many more. In this way, you will be aware of how much you've got left for the remaining costs for the month.

Each whenever we purchase or purchase you must note the date as well as the section. If the purchase has to involve food, leisure, clothing or other items, etc. It must be consistent and precise. It is impossible to leave anything unrecorded, regardless of how small is, as it will not be beneficial. The most important thing is to plan and control. When you're done with each month and every week you'll be able calculate your expenses by category and determine whether you've met your savings goals for the month. This way, you'll be able correct your behavior for the coming month. Numerous examples and posts on forums show the effectiveness of this strategy, which can result in savings of as much as $200 per month, without having to go through the demands.

Saving money in the bank signifies that the bank won't charge you withdrawal charges or in the event that you do not have the minimum amount of money on your bank account by the close of every month. Additionally, these institutions charge interest on your cash in accordance with the amount you've deposited. Naturally, the greater amount you have, the more rate of interest. But you're not going to be able to earn an income by the interest that the bank pays you, since it's not very excessive. It's a different story when you invest in boxes that are referred to as rural or the financial ones that provide the highest rewards for deposits that last over 360 days.

Make sure you pay your bills on time. After a certain period this can negatively affect your credit scores and credibility. Make sure to note it down in your journal and use an alarm program for reminders of days you've been late with payment.

Be cautious when closing accounts. Contact the bank via phone and later in person. Make sure that there aren't outstanding commitments or outstanding debts with the institution. The report states that accounts that haven't been properly closed create debts. It is advised to put off the creation of a new account and the closing of the previous one to ensure that pay-roll and receipts are correctly transferred into the account that you have opened. Take your time, as the cancelling a card can take up to a month.

Prepare for big purchases. It doesn't matter if it's a house or vehicle, or another important purchase, credit scores that are high let borrowers get lower interest rates and greater credit limits. Make an effort to increase your credit score in just six months. In order to do this, you need to think ahead about when you would like to purchase.

Do not get into debt that is beyond your financial capacity. Do not take on loans you cannot pay back within 60 days. In your monthly earnings it is recommended to only use an amount between 30-40 percent for the repayment of the debts.

The process of overcoming Credit Card Debt

Before you begin take the time to read all conditions and terms of your credit card attentively. By doing this you can avoid disappointment , and you will be alert to what's to come.

Do not withdraw cash through credit cards. Particularly, for the purpose of paying off credit card or other loans. Combine your credit cards. An excellent use is an afternoon filled with possible purchase that is payable or a meal which you can cancel right away to ensure that your credit card is in good standing. Contact the bank to negotiate and be firm when applying in requesting new loans.

Be cautious when combining private and business accounts because personal loans only assist you up to a certain point and your company will be able to overexceed the financial resources that are linked the assets you own, this could reduce the stability of your finances. If you take out business loans they give your business the possibility of building an impressive financial record which can allow you to obtain bigger and more complicated credit in the coming years. They offer better terms with rates that range between 8 and 12 percent, as opposed to the rates of a person whose proportions vary between 45 and 50% per year.

Maintain Your Credit Histories This Way

Block the cards, but do not overspend on shopping.

Make use of your account. Purchase items and pay the full balance every month. By doing this you can keep your balance-limit ratio at a low level. Utilizing less than your credit limit can help improve your score on credit. You can do a little shopping you do.

Make sure you pay your bills promptly. Creditors look over your payment history to determine your credibility. Be sure to remember this.

You must keep your job, business or your the primary residence for two years or longer. The lenders take this information into consideration when determining your financial stability. It is a good idea to be responsible even for an independent business. It is a fact that today having a steady job isn't enough. The creation of a business earns you money by virtue of your experience.

Keep reviewing your credit reports. This way, you can spot mistakes and fraudulent activity. Inform us of any issues immediately. Never neglect it. Set aside some time to go through the report on the Internet.

We must also mention that among the items you can purchase with your credit card is hotels, airfare, cruises and other forms of travel because they provide benefits that aid in saving money as well as safeguard you from financial losses. When you purchase a new smartphone using credit cards offers extended warranties as well as protection against damage and theft during the first 90-120 days after purchasing the product.

Additionally the credit card can be handy to pay in advance for products or services you'll get in the future. In the event that the delivery of the item or service that you have paid for is delayed, your card issuer will pay customers for their purchase. With certain credit cards, you may earn additional points and miles to pay for electric, cable and

Internet charges. Remember this: the credit card isn't the loan you get from your bank since it's an amount the bank loans you and you have to repay. It is not a way to purchase items in installments of a number of times, instead, you should pay between three and six. In this way, you don't make more of your purchases.

Chapter 9: 14 Of The Most Destructive Items On Your Credit Report

We will look at ways to minimize the most damaging negative elements that could impact your credit report. Certain of these subjects are quite complex and are beyond the scope of this guide to offer financial and legal guidance on what to do about these problems. But, we do examine various options to tackle these problems.

Despite all the facts available that is available on Internet and advice from other sources that are not trustworthy There isn't a silver solution that can easily and immediately remove all negative information off your credit reports. There isn't a magic formula that only a handful of smart people across the world are aware about. There isn't a credit repair company that is able to guarantee its services also. The reason for this is that, when negative information is correct there is no way to oblige the agency that is reporting it neither the IRS or the credit bureau to eliminate the information. You can request it and you may try some loopholes that could work however you are not able to make it happen.

The solutions listed in this article have been successful for different individuals; however, they may not be effective for everyone in every situation. You must determine for yourself what is best for you.

The good news is that almost every day people can have these damaging things removed from their credit reports. You can too with a little effort and, in some instances you may have luck.

1. Late Payments - A late payment can result in an indebtedness mark on your credit report. The most frequently reported negative mark on credit reports. Things like being late by 30 days on your mortgage payments are serious and could cause a significant decrease on your score. Pay history is around 35 percent on your score, which means the late payment will result in a negative effect.

If you're currently behind in payments, ask your creditor if they could negotiate an amount that is lower than the settlement amount that includes the removal of the late payments from your credit report after you've settled your obligation. If they insist on the full amount , then you might have to catch up before doing anything else.

If you are unable to pay the late payment, contact the creditor to see to negotiate an alternative payment plan that will remove the late payment details after you've completed a specific amount of installments, like the first 12 monthly installments for the year to come.

If they want to pay to pay the entire amount first the next step is to make sure you are current with the amount due. When you're current with your payment and have made them, you can call the creditor and argue your case to eliminate the late payment negative information. In the event that you are in lengthy partnership with them inform them know. If you are in a short time relationship make sure you focus on your excellent performance up to the present situation. The goal is to show them that you're a loyal customer and wish to keep being a great customer. Be courteous and calm and request them to remove any negative information that they put on your credit report. If they're willing, ask for the agreement written. The contact information of their company is in your credit file beneath "Creditor Contacts."

When a late-paying transaction is listed in your credit history, the information can be there for as long as seven years. If the payment was made fully, it could simply say "paid" to your credit score.

2. Collections - A credit card account is typically transferred to collections within six months after the initial missed payment, and it will stay on your credit record for about seven years. If you settle the entire amount due, the status of your account will be changed in your credit file in the form of "paid collections." In the event that you pay less than that, the credit report may show "settled to less than full balance."

3. Charge-offs - the majority of charge-offs result from not paying your credit card invoice for several months. In most cases, after a period of 180 days without payment the creditor (after getting your credit reports with numerous payments that are not made or late) will mark the account as an expense on their books and will also close the account.

4. Short-sales

A short-sale is that you can negotiate with the bank concerning how to sell your home.

When the lender is willing to short-sales (and they typically are, since it's better than foreclosure) the bank will cooperate with you and with the buyer to establish the most mutually agreeable price for the house.

5. Modifications to loans - a modification of a loan is where the loaner agrees with the borrower to alter some or all of the initial conditions for the loan. These modifications could include extending the term of loan altering the rate of interest or altering the amount of the monthly payment. This allows homeowners to maintain their home when they are unable to make mortgage payments at their current rate. The way the modification of your loan affects your credit score will depend on the particulars and the terms of modification.

6. Judgments- Judgments can be complicated because they cover the entire spectrum and you're typically dealing with the system of the court. The first thing you need to be aware of is that the courts usually don't give judgment details to credit bureaus. They obtain it through third-party sources, or via their own searches of public information. They then document it in the way they think is

appropriate. It is therefore possible that a judgment could be reported in a different way (or completely) by every credit bureau. This means that you might be required to deal with every credit bureau in a different way also.

7. Wage garnishment - If you owe money , and the creditor sues you and gets an award against you the creditor may have your wages taken straight from the employer. The law in the United States limits the amount that can be garnished up to 25 percent of your take home pay, minus taxes. A wage garnishment judgment may be recorded on your credit file up to seven years.

8. Car repossessions is when loan payments are not made and the lender takes possession of the vehicle. The creditor then has to sell the vehicle and, if the purchase price is not enough to cover the remaining loan, the creditor could decide to let the debt go, or seek the remaining amount from you. The remaining amount could comprise such expenses as charges for repossession storage, towing, costs for cleaning the vehicle and preparing it for sale or auction, registration fees, the cost to auction or sell the vehicle,

and many additional. In certain cases it could be more expensive to allow the car to be taken away than to make payments.

9. The term "student loan" refers to a loan is used to serve the reason of paying tuition, housing , and textbooks when the student is at school. This is different from a typical loan in that the rate of interest for a student loan is generally lower, and the borrower can put off payments until no longer in the school.

10. Medical Costs-The effects of medical bills on family budgets is often overlooked. But, it's one of the major issues in America currently. According to reports published nationally that in 2013 56 million Americans were struggling to pay medical bills, 15 million spent their savings for medical expenses, 1.7 million declared bankruptcy due to medical expenses, and almost half of late payments resulted from medical bills. If you're among the people mentioned above, it is clear that you're in a lot of friends.

11. Tax Liens Tax Liens an instrument that the government employs to notify other creditors that they have an obligation to your home due from tax debts that have not been paid. Due to the decline in the economy and the

rise in tax liens, they have increased over the last few years. Taxpayer Advocate found that Taxpayer Advocate found that the IRS had filed more than 300,000 tax lien claims in 2013 all by itself.

12. A bankruptcy is without doubt the most damaging thing you can do on your credit report. Indeed, your score can fall as much as 300 points following bankruptcy.

13. Foreclosure - Managing the financial and legal aspects of foreclosure is not the subject of this guide, therefore we advise you to get expert advice before making any financial decision that is significant. There could be even low cost housing counselors in your neighborhood who can assist you on your options as well.

14. Closed Accounts - A lot of people believe that if an account is shut down or inactive, that it doesn't affect your credit rating. But, if the account is closed when in debt, the deficiency remains in your credit file for a period of up to 7 years. Even when it was in good financial standing at the time it was closed, it can have a negative impact on your credit score. The lenders want to see the long-term history of your credit and the

smallest percentage of available credit being utilized. Closing an account could reduce your credit history as well as increase the proportion of credit available. If you're concerned of having too much accounts open Be selective when choosing the ones you close. Be sure there's no balance left at the time of closing and ask for confirmation from the bank that your account is closed.

If the account that was closed has a balance and you want to call the creditor who originally made the request and agree to the settlement. Let them know that you are prepared to settle a certain percentage of the debt , if they're willing to take any negative credit information off your report. The greater the amount of debt and the higher likelihood they'll be willing to negotiate and offer a portion of the debt. The older the debt, the greater leverage you will have in the negotiation. In the event that the debt is more than three years old, you could offer 25percent of the amount due; for the age of two to three years Try 50%, and for less than 2 years, try 75 percent. The results will be more favorable when you pay the debt in one lump amount. If you are required to pay for a loan at a later date, you may need to pay a greater percentage, or even the whole amount. Whatever the amount of your settlement ensure that you have a signed statement from the company that they erase the negative information from your credit report in exchange for the settlement.

Chapter 10: Repairing Your Self-Credit Step And Strategies

Pay To Delete Strategy

If you find derogatory information on your credit report, you may choose to pay the credit balance that you haven't paid in the event that the creditor agrees to remove the items on your credit file. Don't accept a $0 balance to appear within your credit reports because it can tarnish your reputation. According to the rule of thumb the less is more rule in this area; the less items you'll find here and the more beneficial for you. This technique is based on the notion that your credit report does not show if you've suffered from any poor credit in the derogatory item section. This is a way to enhance your credit rating. The idea behind this is to make sure that the amount you are willing to pay is not listed as your date of activities. If the creditor is only concerned about their cash, why would they want to inform the world that you've finally paid?

In the majority of cases, creditors usually erase debts within 2 years of perpetual default and then this information is sold to a collection agency for a few pennies of one dollar. That means that collection agencies will get away with it in the event that you pay less than you are supposed to pay. Whatever you pay, they'll continue to make profits! This means they are open to discussions about the option to pay to delete, since they aren't losing anything otherwise.

* Therefore, you should only employ the pay to delete method at this stage and not alternative. The only alternative for the collection agency is to get a judgement which is costly therefore you may gain in this case.

Use this technique to avoid new negative items appearing on your credit report, which could damage your credit rating. consumer.

Additionally, as lenders will typically sell the same information to different collection firms, you may likely find yourself with the same debt that is being filed by multiple companies. make use of pay to delete to remove them from your record.

You could also employ this method if you've had difficulty getting things off your credit report through other strategies. The decision to dispute the matter could create a cycle that can be time-consuming and exhausting You don't want to fall into this cycle.

If you are aware of the best time to apply this method, knowing how it all operates is vitally important. First, make sure that you have an acceptance letter in the event that they are in agreement with your terms; don't make payments without a letter! Once you've agreed, it will take approximately 45 days for the subsequent credit reports to be provided through your credit monitoring service. They are legally able to begin the process of deletion therefore, don't settle for anything less than an update of the balance. It's either deletion or not. If they attempt to delay the process by saying they are unable to delete, inform them that it will take approximately 5 minutes to complete the Universal Data Form. Do not be concerned if one business does not agree with your requirements, because another will likely appear and accept the deal.

In all likelihood, what are they gaining in keeping your debt when you're prepared to make payments? Be aware that the documents will only be there for 7 years, so if 2 years that are past the companies are forced to accept that you could simply allow the seven years go by! But don't use this as a reason for not paying off your debts as creditors may pursue you in court to force you to pay the outstanding amount. The goal of this process is to make sure that any negative experience you've had with one particular creditor does not cause other creditors make bad decisions for you.

Be cautious not to be too aggressive with creditors that have a lot at stake in the process, especially recent creditors as they will likely be able to sue you. It is best to engage with those creditors who are prohibited by statutes of limitation from being able to sue your in court. It is not a good idea to get you in legal troubles and increase the severity of your issues. Be as smart as you can, and make the correct decisions to improve your credit in the earliest time possible.

Pay-to-delete isn't the only option you have You can also employ different strategies to restore your credit.

Verify to see if there are FDCPA (Fair Law of Debt Collection) For violations of the FDCPA (Fair Debt Collection Practices Act).

The law is specific about what collection agencies can and cannot do and cannot do in the area of debt collection is concerned. For example:

* They should not contact you more than once the course of a day, unless they are able to demonstrate that the call was accidental called using their computerized systems.

* They are not able to call you until 8.00.am as well as after 9.00pm.

* They can't make threats, insults or shout at you to get you to settle any outstanding obligations.

* They can't inform anyone except your spouse about the reason they're calling you.

The best method to accomplish this is to inform them that you will be recording their calls.

* They can't access more funds from your account that you have authorized when they make an ACH.

* They're also not permitted to send letters of collection if you've already issued them an order to cease and desist.

If you can show that the collection agencies are not complying with the law, you must make a formal complaint to the company and request that your lawyer submit proof of the violation; you may then ask that any unpaid dues be repaid. It is important to realize that law enforcement is your side in these situations; however when violations are serious the collection firms might be compelled to pay fines up to $10,000 for the violations.

If your debt is less that this figure, then you may be well on the way to clearing your debt since the companies are more likely to pay your debt rather than pay the penalty. Any offense against the Fair Debt Collection Practices Act can result in the possibility of a fine up to $1000. This is due to you, so do not think of it as a matter that isn't going to be anything in terms of as the repair of your credit is concerned.

Find errors within your Credit Reports

Your credit report needs to be error-free. Even the tiniest error like reporting the incorrect date of the last activity in your credit file could be enough to ruin your credit. The last date you did your activity can have a significant impact on your credit score. If the date for writing off differs from the date that was recorded, you may contest the record to have it rectified to reflect the actual credit status. Keep in mind that credit bureaus will typically verify that the negative entry is correct , even if that isn't the case, so they will not take away the inaccurate item.

It is essential to work to put them on the right path. To ensure they comply with the law, you need to be clear that the law requires that they have a the majority of their processes set up to make sure that mistakes do not occur. Thus, the simple evidence of confirming the original mistake isn't enough. Inform them of notice (Summons) and make a complaint to make them aware that you're committed to the issue. When they know the gist of your stand and your position, they'll put in efforts to be a good example. But bureaus don't wish to see any case go to court as this could eventually prove the system is ineffective or unsound, which means that they could have more serious issues.

Therefore, you must try to get your message across clearly so that they know you are serious about business. A simple exchange of emails won't suffice and you should give them specifics on how convincing your case will be. They will be able to comprehend the situation and choose to assist you avoid going to court. This, in turn, will benefit you in causing them to investigate deeper into the matter. But, this approach can only be effective if are confident that an error was caused. It is also necessary to prove it for the error and not simply declare that it is an oversight.

Request proof of the original Invoice

If you're sure that your credit card been cancelled due to the late payment, it's very likely that the card issuers (Capital One or Citibank) can't locate the original bills within 30 days, and is required by law to provide. This lets you have the information you are disputing deleted from your credit report, as if the event never took place.

Another method is to ask for the original contract you signed to be supplied for proof that proves that you had the credit card opened at the beginning. When you request this, don't simply request "verification" as this only allows the collection company to "verify" that they have actually received a collection request on a credit card that has the name of yours on it. So, as an etiquette be sure to state in writing that you would like to show proof of the debt , including statement of billing for the last few months as well as the original contract you signed at the time of opening an account with a credit card.

You must pay the original creditor.

If your debt is sold by collection companies, you likely be at risk of having new items appear on your credit reports, which could harm your credit score. But, you can prevent the process by writing a check for the complete payment of the outstanding amount to the creditor who originally owed you the money after which you simply provide a receipt of the payment to the collection agency you chose and ask the agency to remove any offensive information they've reported on the credit file.

It's always an excellent idea to stay in contact with your lender or creditors. In reality the majority of these companies are fully prepared to defraud you and implement plans to make your report show a low credit score. It's up to you to remove those "middlemen" and then make your own payment. You may also agree to agreements to transfer a part of the sum to the creditor in full payment for the amount (the pay-to-delete strategy).

In accordance with Federal law, when an initial creditor accepts any of the payments as a complete payment to pay any outstanding debt the collection agency must to eliminate the debt they declared. This is only in the event that the creditor has accepted the payment. It's possible for some check you make to the creditor who originally issued the check that you have paid to them to return to the original creditor.

Elimination of Requests From The Report

Hard Inquiries

When a potential creditor or lender asks to check the credit history of yours, it makes an inquiry to the bureau responsible for credit. The same happens on your credit report. There are two kinds of inquiries: whether they are soft or hard inquiry.

If you are applying for a credit line and the lender looks at your credit report in order to determine whether you're a possible candidate, it is a difficult inquiry. An inquiry that is hard will always appear within your credit reports. A hard inquiry can affect your credit score overall. If you are applying for a credit card, mortgage auto loan, mortgage, or any other credit type the lender will look up your score as well as credit reports. The lender conducts this check without your permission. They will review your credit report through any or all one of the leading credit bureaus. Because this inquiry is linked to a credit request, these are considered hard inquiries, and will be reported on the credit reports of your creditors. Since they appear within your credit reports, they will affect the credit rating of yours.

Let's take a take a look at how hard inquiries impact your credit rating. If you have numerous hard inquiries on your credit report in the span of a few days, it's a red signal for prospective lenders. Inquiries that are hard, particularly multiple ones, could indicate that you're planning to open multiple accounts. When you begin to open multiple accounts, it indicates your financial situation is in desperate need of money and your financial situation isn't very good. It could also indicate that you're spending too much. It can also affect your credit report and your score on credit.

You might think that one could have numerous inquiries regarding credit since they're looking for the most affordable deal on loans. Credit rating models will consider this possibility. The majority of them will accept multiple inquiries within the timeframe of credit lines that are based on the purchase of a car or mortgage loan. Multiple inquiries regarding an individual credit item will be considered as one inquiry and result in a less significant impact to your credit score. In most cases, you won't be denied credit due to the quantity of inquiries that appear on the credit file. It's because a difficult inquiry is just one of many variables which are considered in generating your credit report and credit score.

Hard inquiries will remain showing up on credit reports for approximately two years, however as time goes by the impact of them diminishes. If you do have a lot of hard inquiries in a brief time frame, it is not an excuse to deny the credit of the lender. Your credit score along with the frequency of your payments are other elements to be considered before you're either granted or rejected for the loan.

If the hard inquiry contained in your credit file is true and you are able to have it removed. You may however contest the inquiry if it was initiated without your consent or if you discover an error. If you discover a difficult inquiry from a non-reliable lender on your credit report it's something you should examine immediately. It's usually an indication to identify theft. If you notice any incorrect hard inquiries on your credit report, you are able to file a complaint over the inquiry. After an investigation, if the bureau finds that the hard inquiry is actually inaccurate, then it will be taken off your credit report. In the event of this it will be erased off your credit report.

Soft Inquiries

Soft inquiries occur whenever you look up the credit reports of your loved ones. It is also when you let another person to review your credit report, such as an employer you are considering or a landlord. Sometimes, different companies and financial institutions, may have deals they believe will be beneficial to you. In these cases they'll look over your credit report and decide if they want to approve you for any of these deals. It is also a type of an inquiry with a soft aspect.

Because a soft inquiry does have no direct connection to an application for an additional line of credit they're typically not visible in your credit reports. However, there are some exceptions to this standard. You are the only person who has access to the soft questions. Two exemptions from this policy are listed below.

A company offering insurance may be able to view the questions made by other companies similar to them.

* Any request that is made by debt settlement companies could be shared with current creditors. This is only possible with your prior consent.

Since they were never considered in any credit score models, these won't be a factor in your credit rating. They can be used as a review, but you are not able to contest them, other than those two above mentioned, they are not viewed by any other person.

Management of inquiries

If you're concerned that the hard inquiries could be damaging your credit score then follow the steps below.

Be careful and only apply for credit when you need to.

* If you're looking for a particular credit line, such as auto or mortgage and you are able to need to do your rate comparison in a short time.

Check your credit report on a regular basis to ensure there aren't any false hard inquiries on it.

Begin to manage other factors that affect your score on credit.

If a hard inquiry has taken place without your consent You can then erase it from the credit report. If you didn't have previously known about the inquiry that was made regarding your credit report, or credit score and your credit profile, then you can request it taken off. In some cases, you can also request that these inquiries be removed from your credit report that were made due to the fact that you were pressured to accept an application which you weren't interested in. These are the most common examples of hard inquiries you can eliminate from the credit file.

* Any inquiry initiated without your prior knowledge.

* Any inquiry initiated without your consent.

* Any request that was conducted because of pressure.

* The amount of inquiries in your report is greater than the amount actually made.

If you find an incorrect investigation on your credit file then you should write a letter to the right agency to request its removal. If you're sending a message to remove and want to remove it, you must mail this to your credit bureau and the lender. These are the steps you have to follow.

First step to mail an official letter to end any credit inquiries in writing to both the credit bureau as well as the lender via an authorized mail service. A certified letter will document the date and time of sending the letter and also when it was it was received. This record can be used to prove legality in the event there is a discrepancy. This can be very useful particularly when the recipient is unable to prove that they received the letter.

If you decide to send a request to end the credit inquiry, you have to inform the lender. It is your obligation to inform the lender if you intend to initiate legal proceedings. Don't be surprised by the fact that the lender may not be as prompt to your needs as your credit reporting bureau. This is however a important step that you shouldn't overlook and it's the correct method to get an incorrect hard inquiry taken off your credit report.

When you send your request for removal letter, please make sure you include a copy of your credit report along with it. Make sure you highlight the error on the report, as well as any other inquiries you have made that aren't authorized. Credit bureaus will have access to your account, however it can help the investigators if give them a paper copy.

Be sure that you're making the request to the appropriate authority. If the issue was found on a report that was compiled by Equifax the report does make sense to mail a copy this letter to TransUnion. Below are the addresses of the three main credit bureaus within the U.S.

The process of removing any negative information from your credit report can be long and takes a lot of time. So, if you want rapid results, this procedure is a test of patience. It may seem as if that a few points could be a big difference on your credit rating however, they could increase to a substantial amount if they are not checked. It is therefore essential to be up to date with any inquiries concerning the removal of any negative entries from the credit reports. If you are looking to boost the credit rating of your would like to maintain it make sure that all entries on your credit file are in order.

Note: Making a number of difficult inquiries within a brief time frame is typically an indication that you are filing for bankruptcy. Multiple hard inquiries indicate that you are in the process of running out of money or are already running out of money. It also suggests that your financial standing is extremely unstable. If you are searching for multiple ways of credit simultaneously due to different reasons, this is an indicator of bankruptcies. If you're conducting any difficult inquiries within a short time frame Be aware of this.

How to boost your Credit Score to 100 points

In any event, you can increase your FICO score regardless of whether you are able to have any negative information removed or on the off possibility that you opt to allow the negative items to disappear from your credit report in the normal course. It's also crucial to handle accumulations with care so that you don't accidentally reset the date for the legally-required time limit.

Consider these methods as a key component of your extensive credit fix strategy to make the most of everything and avoid a rash of problems that can cause lasting damage.

1. Review Your Accounts in Collections

Begin by looking at the ongoing balances. They are the ones that have the greatest impact on your credit score on the basis that the older obligations is weighed more heavily. In addition, you should be aware of the type of debt you're taking on.

The medical obligation won't impact your accept as much as other types of obligations. Therefore, you need to focus on non-therapeutic obligations first. Try to pay in full as halfway installments could be reset as to how long they will be reflected for the duration of your credit history.

You could also try to negotiate a settlement deal with the accumulation company to settle the difference between the amount you have to pay. Be aware that you might be required to record the amount which was not paid on your form for assessment, which can result in higher expenses , and perhaps a greater duty rate in the possibility that it forces you into a different payment level.

Another problem with settling delinquent payments can arise if the gathering office acts like you've never ever made an installment. Keep a distance from this technique by having your installment agreements recorded in an original document and keeping copies of all the reports that are associated in the report.

2. Make sure to check your Credit

If you've reviewed your information in accumulations make sure those changes are assessed in relation to on your credit reports. It could take a few months for the data to go off, so you should wait for a few minutes before checking your credit report and FICO score.

If there aren't any positive developments or that the negative aspect is not yet documented the issue, you must record your debate with the credit agency. In the event that you have kept excellent records, you must have the appropriate documentation to meet the requirement to speed up your deliberation.

Quick Tips to Repair Your Credit

Removing negative items from your credit history can result in emotional effects on your credit score, however, it's a process that could take quite a long time.

If you're looking for quick fixes There are two options you can try. Certain are small fixes and others could result in a significant change therefore, make sure to read the full listing to find out which you can try today to repair your credit.

1. Lower Your Credit Utilization Ratio

The closer you get towards maximizing your cards less your FICO score will be.

This is a good sign that squaring the equalizations you have on your charge cards could lower the percentage of your account and boost your score. Make sure you are using cards with the highest adjusts instead of ones that have low adjustments; therefore you could experience up to 100 points increase in just a few months.

3. Request an Increase in Limit Increase on Credit Cards. Limit An increase in the credit limit on Cards

If you're unable to pay for an additional obligation that will reduce the use of your credit, you are eligible for improvement. Contact at least one of your credit card backers to offer to increase the limit of your credit card.

If you don't want to be able to charge more than what you currently are owed, however, you must to reach a higher point, with the aim that your current balance consists less of credit available.

Here's a sample. Let's suppose you have a balance of $5,000 on a credit card that has an amount of $10,000. You'd only use half of your credit. However, in the event that you were to get your credit limit to $15,000, the $5,000 equalization will only make use of 33 percent of your breaking point.

If you are deciding whether to present be your loan manager it is helpful on the possibility that you've made regular punctual installments prior to your first appointment with them. Most likely, they'll appreciate your loyalty to the client enough to allow your credit to be repaid.

4. Sign up to become an authorized user

The process of establishing your profile as a customer takes an extensive amount of time, but there's another option available. Find a friend or family member with an established, stable credit score and ask to become an approved customer on one or more of their accounts. The Mastercard record will then be added to your credit report, and will be surprisingly complete.

There's a risk that comes with this decision If your friend or relative stops making payments or makes an equalization, the negative portions are added to the history of the transaction.

The same way when you have additional adjustments and do not assist in making any payments you're responsible of, the other person's credit may be damaged. This is a fantastic method, but it will require an awareness.

5. Consolidate Your Credit Card Credit Card

Another quick way to repair your credit is by taking out an obligation-solidification advance. It's essentially a close-to-home loan that you use to pay off of your various Mastercards after which you pay only a single monthly amount of the credit.

Dependent on your financial costs Based on your financing costs, you could be able to obtain an excellent bargain on your regular installments by obtaining the lowest rate for advance. Check out pre-endorsements and determine what rates you can qualify for and how they compare when compared to your current rate on your credit card.

No matter if you pay the original investment back on regular installments and if you do, your FICO evaluation will be higher since the portion advances are viewed more positive than spin credit.

6. You can get a credit-developer loan

Credit unions and smaller banks frequently offer credit-manufacturer advance to help people repair their credit. When you get your credit card, those funds are incorporated into a file that you're not able to access.

Then, you begin making regular installments on the amount of your advance. After you've repaid the total credit, the funds are cleared for you to use.

It could appear unusual to earn money you cannot spend, but it's actually a way for the financial institution to be confident that you have the chance to establish yourself as a competent borrower.

If you successfully complete your installments and collect the money, the bank confirms that your installments are on time to credit bureaus to help improve your FICO score.

7. Make use of a tiny portion from your limit on credit

"Credit utilization" is a credit representation of the amount of your credit's breaking point at which you're using. The amount you use impacts your FICO score. Just paying on time is more important.

The majority of experts recommend not going more than 30% on any credit card. Lower is more beneficial for your score. If your Mastercard backer has reported an equalization lower to the credit department and your score will benefit. The score will not be damaged due to your previous high credit use when you've reduced the amount of adjusts.

8. Get a co-signer

If you're having major difficulty obtaining credit, you can ask a family member or friend to sign a co-signed advance or credit card. This is an enormous support you're asking the person put their credit reputation to the side for you, and assume the full responsibility for any reimbursement should you do not pay the amount agreed to. The co-underwriter might also be rejected in the event they seek credit later due to the fact that this information will be scrutinized when assessing their financial history. Use this option with caution and ensure that you are able to repay. If you fail to make this payment, it could damage the reputation of the co-endorser's credit and the relationship between you.

9. Pay as per your time

Make sure you keep your accounts and current credit extensions according to the schedule, every time. Every single aspect affects your financial situation in the same way as your past history of paying on time installments. If you're trying to rebuild credit, you shouldn't be able to fail to pay an installment.

Late payments remain on your credit report for up to seven years. This means that they are more difficult to recover from than the other types of credit slips.

If there are bills that have just been deemed insolvent you should organize them in the areas where your records are not open. The people who gather may be the ones to cause the most noise, however they're not your primary need.

Chapter 11: Perhaps You Have A Need For A Credit Expert

You've learned more about credit systems and the significance of increasing your score or credit scores, and contesting inaccurate entries, and other causes of a low score and ways to repair these. These processes will take some time and energy and many people don't have the time to fix their credit. To accomplish this it is recommended to hire an "credit repair business" which will take care of the job for you paying a small cost for the service.

Credit Repair Companies

Credit repair firms provide assistance in reducing your credit scores. The idea of contacting these firms is seen as the last option as the majority of people try to solve their credit problems on their own but if they're unable, then they'll seeking assistance. The primary function of these businesses is to assist people in repairing their poor credit score and, as such they'll have expert in this subject. They'll have staff who are dedicated to finding the mistakes, providing expert opinions as well as transferring the information. Once you've decided to use their services You can rest easy.

The procedure these firms follow is straightforward. They'll ask for an original duplicate of your credit file (they will only request ones that are obtained by the three top credit agencies , viz. TransUnion, Experian and Equifax) and review it in depth. When they're finished they will search for errors in the entries you could contest. The entries should be addressed as soon as possible and to do this, they'll return as soon as it is possible. When you have received their response and you are able to proceed with the dispute procedure. The dispute team will then contact the credit agencies to dispute any information in your credit report which do not seem to be correct.

They prefer to trust these businesses even when they're unable to spot the errors on their own or have the time or patience to contest the error. They will assist them to speed up the process and finish the task as soon as possible. Even though they don't be able to complete things that are above and beyond your capacity but they can help facilitate a smoother and more efficient process. They'll do it the same manner as you would except you've now contracted the task to these companies.

In Search Of The Most Effective

When it comes to letting an outside person with your personal data It is likely that you'll have a few reservations. This is normal since there is no reason to be concerned about giving their personal details to other people. However, if you locate the right business that is focused on nothing but helping you improve your credit score, and then you can give them your personal information with no worries. However, for this it is important to search for the top firm.

Here are some suggestions to help you select the best company for you.

* Do not be a believer in a company making you pay money without reviewing your credit history. There is no way for a company to charge you until they've completed their task for you.

* Do not trust companies that don't explain your rights in detail or explaining what you

are allowed and not permitted to do while disputing your claim.

* Don't believe a company insisting that you do not call the credit agencies on your own and then claim to assist you.

If your credit card company advises you to take an illegal move, it's ideal to don't pursue the matter further.

These are just a few of the most common criteria you should take into consideration when searching for a company to repair your credit.

Rates, and other information

It is essential to take into consideration the prices being charged by these businesses. If they are over-charging for the service that they offer, it is not worth considering the charges they are charging. It is important to learn from other people what they're paying for credit repair services and also pay the same costs. You should look through the brochure, which lists the various services they provide, as well as an estimate of fees in the event that it is offered. Make sure they provide you with any guarantee. A majority of businesses do not offer anything because it's an opportunity for them. However, if the business is competent enough and has lots of trust in solving any problem , then they could offer you some guarantees.

Also, you should consider the timing they have set to provide their service. It shouldn't be any greater than 1 or 2 weeks. The earlier they start, the more effective. If they provide you with an in-depth analysis, you should wait for some time and it's not too long. Make sure you have the contact information for them. You must have access their addresses and telephone numbers. You have to be able call or visit them anytime. After you have received your report and decide to challenge the entry and pay the company what is due.

Something Bureaus and lawyers don't want You to Be able to

Credit is now a popular American lifestyle. Because of the increased usage of charge accounts as in credit cards as well as other no-money-down incentives, it was necessary to release reports on the credit history of the consumers.

Credit reporting agencies were established to offer the reports. These agencies, commonly known as credit bureaus, comprise organizations that collect information about consumers who use credit and sell it to banks, retailers and credit card companies. They also sell it to finance companies, as well as other lenders. The data is offered in the form of credit reports. They also include an evaluation mark that is positive neutral, negative or negative.

Credit bureaus are able to freely share information between themselves, including information on the average, for all Americans who's ever sought credit. They also share data with other bureaus whenever people movefor instance. When you've got a strong credit history in your area you are able to get credit anyplace in the United States.

Credit bureaus store the information on file that is provided in time by your creditors. However, they do not evaluate how good or poor the credit risk you pose and they don't give any judgement on the ability of you to pay back the loan. It is the prospective creditor, who has requested the file to decide whether or not to give credit. The three main federal credit agencies are responsible for maintain your credit history. They all work independently from each other when it comes to collecting information about you. They are armed with vast databases that keep track of the credit histories of several hundred million people all over the globe.

Experian is the largest , with $4.7 billion in revenue in 2013. Equifax which has $1.9 billion in revenue , is the longest-running of the three agencies, and has information about more than 400 million credit card holders around the world. TransUnion ranks third in the size of credit bureaus across America and has $1.1 billion in revenue.

What do creditors look for?

To establish an outstanding credit score You need to have a solid knowledge of the game of credit. The principle that is most commonly employed to assess your credit worthiness can be called"the 3 C's of Credit. The three C's include:

Character

Your character is determined by how you've dealt with your past transactions. Creditors look at factors as the amount you owe them, how often you take out credit and how frequently you've paid back past debts. They also take into account how long you've been working at your current job, the location of the address you are currently at, and whether or not you own or lease.

Capacity

This will show your financial capacity to pay back your loan. Creditors may ask you to provide information regarding your work experience: Your job title and the amount of duration of time you've been employed in this or your last position and the amount you make.

Capital

Capital refers to your possessions which could be used to secure your loan. The creditor needs to know which property or funds that is not your income that you earn regularly could be used to guarantee the loan. Your assets include your home or car, jewelry as well as bonds and stocks as well as savings and any other valuables.

Credit grantors and lenders employ various combinations of these factors in deciding. Each credit grantor grants credit according to their own policies and standards. One creditor may consider you creditworthy however, another might refuse you credit. If you don't have credit-worthy experience (character) You may still be given credit on the basis of your capacity and capital until you have established a strong credit history.

How do the Credit Bureau and Lawyers Don't Want You To Know

1. You only disputed the error through the furnisher.

If you suspect that your lender is not reporting your information in the credit reporting agency, it could be easier to bypass the credit bureau and just deal directly with your lender. Don't do it.

The credit bureaus would depend heavily on an investigation by a supplier to prove the accuracy of a mistake. In a settlement reached in 2015 in a 2015 settlement with the State of New York, the three major credit bureaus agreed to look into complaints more thoroughly if customers provided evidence to support their claims and an initial assessment was conducted without making any changes.

2. You've lost evidence.

If you submit disputes after disputes with credit-reporting agencies but continue to get nowhere then the next option is to file a lawsuit against the credit bureaus according to experts. (You could even submit an appeal with the Consumer Financial Security Bureau.)

It's unlikely that you'll make it through your lawsuit but in the event that you don't have evidence to prove that the mistake is correct and you've suffered serious harm consumers lawyers claim.

In a myriad of court cases that are reviewed by CreditCards.com many individuals are unable to present their case to an impartial jury due to having not kept enough evidence which could be presented in court to show they've been wronged.

The instance was referred to summary judgment on an appeal by the credit bureau, or information provider, leading to a ruling by the judge, rather than an open trial with a jury.

To present a case to an unconstitutional judgment and to have jurors listen to the case and give you the greatest chances of winning You must prove that there's a plausible divergence in what transpired to the dispute , and also the impact that the outcome had on the outcome for you.

It involves saving records like an official mail receipt which shows your credit agency is able to process your dispute.

"The big three frequently have to either lose or appear to the correspondence of customers," says Leonard Bennett an advocate for consumers with Consumer Litigation Associates in Newport News, Virginia.

"If you have a potential lender informed you that a negative entry led to rejection or approval with the higher rate then get the name and the title of the representative of the lender who told you this and request a document that they have written."

Also, it is necessary to keep all financial documents including any credit denials that you've received. "Those rejections of credit letters prove that the consumer may be affected by the errors in their credit reports."

"Saving your denial of credit letters might be helpful if you have to dispute the behavior of the creditor due to other reasons," says Cary Flitter who is a consumer lawyer and law professor from Philadelphia.

The additional documentation you provide will help to ensure that credit bureaus will immediately correct the error if you contest it, allowing you stay clear of lengthy court processes.

Credit monitoring agencies were known to refuse or not provide evidence to lenders' claims experts. Since 2013 these agencies have been subject to more scrutiny by authorities like the Consumer Financial Protection Bureau and State Attorneys General. They've promised to review their dispute procedure and to take their facts more seriously.

For instance, as in the aftermath of the 2015 deal with the State of New York, employees of the credit bureau are required to verify errors using the information they've submitted, instead of relying on automated dispute procedures.

The employees can accelerate inquiries in the event that an error involves fraud, identity theft, or mixed files , and then providing the supporting documentation to trained employees. In June 2018 credit bureaus will no longer be able to reject your claim if you've already filed a dispute in the past three years.

These laws don't - and cannot be applied to you when you submit your dispute to a credit repair business instead of personally and, therefore, be sure to provide your personal information yourself.

3. You didn't provide enough details regarding your disagreement.

In the event of contesting errors on credit reports the majority of people choose the convenience of filing an action online or via phone.

These agencies marketing this conciseness by advertising via their website how simple it is to utilize their online dispute platforms that also provide you with just enough space to write an e-mail describing the dispute.

Consumer lawyers advise against using the form provided from the credit agency without including additional documentation or a letter describing your dispute could result in losing the case if you needed to bring the credit bureau before a judge.

Credit bureaus are now able to attach additional details to your online dispute explicit.

Instead of writing an elaborate letter to the creditors, the experts suggest to:

* Provide reasons why the data included in your study are incorrect.

* Documentation to prove the error.

If you include the documents in the note (and taking copies of your documents) You make it more difficult for the credit agency to declare that the error was yours because you didn't submit enough evidence the consumer lawyer says.

Experts also suggest you also send copies of the same to the lender who is associated with the error to serve the same reason. They will send any proof that you include in the dispute, which includes additional letters you write detailing the dispute. It could be beneficial to send an additional letter to the provider, in case.

Data providers and lenders are also being advised of The Consumer Financial Protection Bureau that they should look into consumer disputes more carefully as they have done previously.

Furthermore the 2015 agreement in 2015 with the State of New York allows credit bureaus to monitor providers with greater vigor and to punish providers who are not following the proper procedures. So, the company is also more likely to properly investigate the issue when you give them enough evidence to prove that the information they offer is incorrect.

4. Also, you did not follow the conditions of the arrangement to the credit bureau.

If you've recently requested an online credit report or opted to get the "free report" from one of the three major credit bureaus, then you've probably missed the terms that appear at the end of the page. Most people do.

This is a big mistake. Certain credit bureaus, like TransUnion also have arbitration clauses in their conditions of service.

That means that if you purchase your credit report on the internet and discover a mistake, you are still able to contest the error. But, if you do disagree with the manner in which the credit bureau dealt with the dispute and want to bring Office to the court, the credit bureau might try to legally apply the arbitration clause and require you to surrender the right to argue your case to an impartial jury or join in a class-action lawsuit against Office. Office.

It can be harder to establish your case and get loss if you've been financially harmed, according to experts.

In the case of arbitration the dispute will be handled by an arbitrator who is a single person, selected by the arbitration group chosen by credit bureaus and it is the responsibility of the arbitrator to decide the matter. If you don't agree with the arbitrator's decision the decision is not yours to appeal.

If you get the credit report of an agency which enforces an arbitration clause Be sure to submit an opt-out notice to the credit department in the first 30-60 days after receiving the report, according to the agreement of the business.

Depending on the place clause on the site of the Office In addition, you may be able claim the arbitration clause isn't legally binding because it wasn't evident that it was applicable on the report that you bought.

In the U.S. in March 2016. In March 2016, the Court of Appeals held that the TransUnion arbitration clause in the web service agreement was not legally binding because the Office did not explain to users that the acquiring of the TransUnion credit score immediately bound the customers to arbitration. It is recommended to opt out from the arbitration clause completely.

Always, remember to examine the terms and conditions that the credit bureau has, if you're going to work with them in the near future, even if there wasn't an arbitration clause last time you've checked the terms.

Presently, some credit bureaus aren't requiring customers to arbitrate their issues with the dispute procedure. For instance, Equifax and Experian now declare in their conditions of service that the arbitration clauses of their companies don't apply to Fair Credit Reporting Act cases. But, this may change if the credit company remains under less pressure from activists and regulators. The increased pressure imposed by credit bureaus during their administration under the Obama administration already started to decrease. In November of 2017 the Trump administration was required to pass to pass a Consumer Financial Protection Bureau regulation which would have stopped credit bureaus and financial institutions from implementing arbitration clauses that prohibit individuals from joining in class action lawsuits.

Under the new administration under the new administration, the CFPB showed less capacity to manage financial firms effectively. This means that certain credit bureaus may be enticed to revisit arbitration agreements with a wider scope.

Whatever the current political situation, it's an excellent idea to keep an habit of looking up the words whenever you receive an credit report or initiate an online dispute.

5. You were listening to the debt collector.

It is not possible to challenge the true information on your credit reports or expect credit agencies not to remove the information. You may, however, make credit bureaus accountable in accordance with the Equal Credit Reporting Act if they fail to adhere to the deadline for repaying your credit card.

Negative information is legally required to be removed from the report within seven years. Insolvency could be listed on your report for as long as 10 years.

If you find a account that's on your credit report, but it is older than seven years you may challenge this debt with the credit bureaus, and demand that it be cancelled. You can also take action against any debt collector who has threatened to take action against you over the debt when it has passed its expiration date.

The date of expiration for the legal term for the debt must give you to defend any claim after the time limit has passed. This tactic works only in the event that you don't accidentally enforce your debt again after speaking to a debt collector states Paul Stephens, Privacy and Advocacy Director at the Privacy Rights Clearinghouse.

"There's an issue of a major magnitude in this particular area," says Stephens. Debt collectors can also sell accounts to each other, and sometimes debt collectors divulge incorrect schedules, leading to for the account to remain open more than it ought to be.

"That's what we refer to as"debt re-engineering,"" the expert states. It's not allowed as a result of the Equal Credit Reporting Act, and you're entitled to challenge it.

However, if you get the call of a debt collector, and accept to pay a part of the debt that is not paid you could theoretically start the debt restriction clock and decrease your ability to defend yourself effectively.

"Debt collectors will continue to call you and harassing them," Stephens says. "They could be able to get you in an emotional or vulnerable point and, at that point of depression, you may commit to entering into a repayment plan or maybe take on the debt."

The debt collector could be able to sue you and get a judgement against you for the debt you could have had the chance to erase from your credit report for good.

Right Mindset for Credit Management

1. Understanding Your Current Mental State

Before you begin making any changes, it is important to determine where your mental state is at the moment. Consider the way you feel when you think over your debt on your credit card since this can tell you more about your attitude than you realize.

If you're like many people, you're feeling dissatisfied with your situation. How you ended up in debt with your credit card will be contingent on what you're saying to yourself. You could, for instance, be upset and blame yourself getting yourself into debt. You may be asking yourself, why you allowed this to happen.

Whatever you see regarding your present mindset You must acknowledge it and comprehend the reasons behind your feelings. It is also important to realize that it's fine that you feel this since it can assist you in reaching the debt-free mentality.

2. The burden of debt is not a burden But it is an obstacle

There's a distinction between an obstacle and a burden. If you're faced with a problem that you are facing, you must take it on; there is no escape. But you can find a solution to overcome the obstruction. Therefore, it is essential consider the debt as a hurdle. It's something is manageable through the correct steps. Also, it is something you can prevent yourself from repeating the same mistake.

Consider a few minutes to think of ways you could make an effort to eliminate your credit card debts as an obstruction. For instance, if you are making a minimum of $75 monthly payment you've been making, what percentage of that is going towards interest and charges? If you find that this amount is only $35, you need to consider the options to raise your monthly payment to $110. This will permit you to make more than your minimum monthly payment. Additionally it allows you to contribute $75 to your balance, with 50% of the amount going toward charges and the remaining half towards your balance.

3. Don't Lose Gratitude!

It is possible to be angry. We frequently see others enjoying the luxury of life, whether through the purchase of a brand-new car or taking a trip. It is possible to feel angry since they can purchase new clothes. One of the most effective ways to overcome the negative attitude associated with financial debts is to let go of your anger and instead focus on the positive.

Take a look around your home and look around and see the many wonderful things you have. Consider the blessings you have with regard with your loved ones, family members and everyone else present in your life. It's not always necessary to think about the larger things. Sometimes, just looking at the small things can be equally beneficial. For instance, you might feel a sense of gratitude when your child smiles at you a smile as they are playing at their toy.

If you have trouble feeling grateful One of the best strategies is to record the things you are thankful for each and each day. Keep a journal and write down the things that has made you feel happy. Also, you can discuss the negative events occurred, however, try to figure out ways to take the lessons learned or transform the negative into something positive.

4. Accept Responsibility for the debt you owe

There's a huge distinction between blameing yourself for the credit card debt and accepting responsibility for it. The main difference is the kind of attitude you're in. For example, if you're asking yourself what could you have done to be foolish enough to get several credit cards, you're blamed for the situation. Instead, you should be accountable, which means that you can say something similar to this: "I know I got myself into debt from credit cards due to taking out excessive credit cards. What can I do now to start paying off that credit card bill?"

Being accountable helps you get in a positive mindset since it allows you to understand that even though you did make a mistake, you have a clear understanding of what went wrong and are now ready to address the issue. Additionally be sure to think about how you can avoid repeating the same mistake. No matter how you manage to get yourself free of debts from credit cards they will continue appear tempting.

5. Stop looking at Debt-Free as a solution to your Problem

Another step to make to prepare your mental attitude to get free of financial debt, is not thinking about getting debt-free as a solution to your issue. In reality, there may be more than one cause the reason you're in debt. While you'd prefer not to be blame, you must be accountable for your errors.

Write down all ways you could be free from debt. It could mean you have to close all your credit card accounts and develop a plan to pay the balance promptly It could be that you need to find a new job to pay your debts rapidly. Instead of thinking of being debt-free as the sole option, consider it as an end result. It is essential to make in debt or enjoying financial independence your primary aim. You must work towards coming up with a set of steps that can aid you in reaching your goal.

Let's say, for instance, that you're a student at college who has opened 5 credit cards. You're about to graduate and you realize that you have to begin paying off your debts that are smaller since you'll be paying back student loan debt in the near in the near future. So, you determine that your top alternatives is to eliminate your credit cards and not ever again make use of them. So, you consider ways to repay your five credit cards within a single year.

Then, you consider the amount of tips you earn from working as waitress. In general, you take home between $100 and $300, based on the time of the day and the amount of work. You know that you can spend all your money to pay off your credit card. This allows you to reduce your debts faster. When you have done the math, you will realize that all of credit cards you have will be paid completely at the point that your student loans begin to be payment. With your plan you began to envision the goal of being debt-free and free from credit cards as an result, rather than your goal. In this way you were able to find a sensible solution that is effective in the event that you're in a position to implement the plan throughout the year.

The mindset of getting out of debt

Make a Game Plan and stick to it

You must set goals and develop a strategy to eliminate debt. Although you don't need to make a list of your goals it is an excellent idea since it can help you stay focussed on what you must to accomplish.

For instance, you realize the fact that you've got five credit cards that are completely maxed out. In fact, you're close to exceeding the limit for all of them. This could result in the credit card company charge you an over-limit charge. You are aware that this is only going to create an additional amount of debit on your credit cards. You decide you must pay more than your minimum monthly payment for these credit cards first.

Reframe Your Ideas

Another important step to take in your mental outlook to get out of debt is turning your negative thoughts to positive ones. This is among the main reasons why you should be grateful for the things you have in your life, which includes your debit card balance. Although this may seem difficult at the moment, it's crucial to recognize that it is a life lesson you're learning. Actually, by getting control of your credit card debt you'll be able be in control of your spending and attain financial freedom. Additionally your more unfavorable you appear and the more difficult it will be to stick to your goals and set budgets.

Make a list of reasons to get out of debt

Resolving credit card debt isn't going to be an easy task. In reality, you'll require steps to remain on track, as there may be moments when you are frustrated or doubt your ability to get free of the debt. One method to combat this is creating the reasons behind seeking to eliminate debt. The list could include any idea that pops into your thoughts. For instance, you might declare that you would like to own your own home in the near future. You could also write that you would like to be debt-free in two years. Another motive could be that your kids are going to college within five years and you'd like to be able to assist them. No matter what you're attempting to accomplish; the most important thing is that they're your motivations to get out of the debt.

Know that People Rely on You

If you are a parent then you should think about the many individuals who depend on your earnings. It's much simpler to to buy diapers, groceries, or any other household goods you'll need, without having to think about what kind of you're putting yourself into. Instead you can pay with the debit card you have or in cash and not have to think about it again.

Automate Payments

Each credit card company allows the setting up of automated payment through their website. Some companies will even enable automatic payments over the phone. Whatever you have to accomplish, make sure you take the time to setup these payment options. This will allow you to ensure that the charges are paid. It is important to should avoid cancelling or delaying your automatic payments since it is a common alternative. It is a feature you can include in your budget, meaning you're less likely make a decision to cancel.

Find ways to keep You Invigorated

When you're drafting your plan to eliminate debt it is important to include strategies that will keep you engaged. It could be that you check your progress each month to determine how much of your debit card balance has reduced. If, for instance, you own five credit cards, and you are paying them $100 each month, you'll find that they've decreased by around 200 dollars every 2 months. If you take this all together it will reduce the total debt on your credit cards by 1,000 dollars. You may decide to keep track of your progress on an Excel spreadsheet using your computer or journals. Take note of the amount you owe at the time you make a payment and take note of the new amount next time you pay.

Be Sure You Are able to Do It

Sometimes, it is difficult to carry our debt-free strategy because we think we're not capable of achieving it. It's important to recognize you will have occasions when you're feeling this way. There will be times you are feeling like you cannot remain focused on paying down your debt. It is possible to look around and realize that you have 2 years' worth of debt from credit cards that you need to pay off, while the other bills continue to accumulate.

Establish a Reward System

It is likely that you'll have to struggle to maintain your motivation to get out of the debt that you incur from time to time. It might not be because you're looking to buy something you cannot afford or even afford, but it could be due to becoming tired of looking at the amount of money you owe on credit cards.

Financial Freedom

If you currently have credit cards and have accrued expenses that are greater than your earnings and you are unable to pay them, then your monthly installments will be difficult to manage without impacting the budget needed to maintain the essential expenses, like the variable costs which are crucial to your daily life. At this point, that you'll need the creation of a strategy to clear the debts that plague you to ensure that it doesn't impact your needs and will be able to repair your credit score.

In this regard you could look at the following recommendations for getting free of credit card indebtedness:

You must stop using for credit card, particularly ones that require greater interest rates. Be sure to cut them with scissors to protect yourself and your freedom. It is best not to carry around items that is not used.

Naturally, you must not stop making payments on the monthly installments of your credit cards . If you need to, to reach this, you should contact the banks and financial institutions to negotiate a renegotiation of the debt. They will be able to negotiate monthly payments that will be used to amortize the debt.

If you have an extension on your credit card, it is necessary to stop the permanent or temporary use of the credit card to associates or relatives of yours All will benefit over all of your credit history.

You should prioritize your expenses, and if needed to do so, only for the job that permits you to use credit cards that provide higher benefits. Additionally, you may receive offers in the event of being required to travel only to job.

Because you can't make payments to your credit card in time, and your income doesn't permit it, you should consider alternatives that permit you to make a new income. Do not make the mistake of taking on new debts to settle the debt that you have already.

The extravagant and leisure or recreational expenses you typically add to your credit cards must be cancelled for the duration of credit recovery or the payment of debts that are delinquent.

When you are preparing to make another time using the credit card, be sure to be aware about the interest rate, taxes you have to pay and the ones that are part of your utility. At the moment, it is always less more.

Your commitment to credit record is entirely yours to make and is your sole responsibility. Don't think there are magical solutions that will get you out of the debts that you have made.

Remember, the improvement of your credit score is contingent on the degree of commitment you've made to managing your finances. It is important to program your expenses by creating an budget that allows you to depending on your income, make expenditures.

If you decide to delegate this responsibility, you won't alter your lifestyle and will therefore remain in a state of uncontrolled spending that could place you at risk and hinder you from rebuilding your credit score. Don't ever spend money on a credit repair service to complete work that is your sole responsibility. These agencies typically employ untrue or illegal methods. You may be facing more trouble than the benefits.

Limit the opening and use of accounts at stores since it can negatively impact your credit score in the short long, medium and short term. Make sure you only use credit cards issued from banks and financial institutions that have a good reputation. Additionally, avoid applying more than one third of your credit line in the event that you aren't sure you can afford to pay it the full amount in the same month. Don't leave your debts unpaid over the course of your next month believing you'll be able to cover it on a monthly income that's not guaranteed.

Some companies offer free credit reports but will charge fees for monitoring. They invite you to sign for a free report, then ask you to provide your credit cards number and instantly switch you over to a paid option following a trial. If you don't end your subscription during this time then you'll be charged monthly to use their service.

If you require specific information regarding the local agencies for credit reportage, or any other aspect of credit rating where you live, you should contact the appropriate agencies in your country.

The current financial situation is shifting in every country, and, naturally, the economic situation in certain countries may not be favorable particularly for small and micro business entrepreneurs. They can't access bank loans, and have to rely on informal lenders, which weakens their capacity to finance and grow due to the fact that the interest rates they charge increase in a steady manner, often surpassing the return rates produced by their business rather than encouraging growth, frequently, they ended up decapitalizing them. To counter this, it's better to rely on trusted people or government organizations for support with credit or refinancing.

Personal or Corporate Credit Card?

In the past previously, you can choose to make use of the credit card you have at home in lieu of the business credit card to make the majority of your purchases. If you're still trying to decide whether you want to keep your personal credit card or opt for a business account there are some aspects to take into consideration.

It is possible to do better using a business credit card If:

You're a new entrepreneur looking to improve the trustworthiness of your company's credit.

* You manage a business that has expenses that require a higher credit limit.

* Your expenses are aligned with the reward categories that business cards can offer.

* You do not need to worry about the low credit limit.

A personal credit card may be the best option for you in the following situations:

* You operate sole proprietorship in which the business expenses do not exceed the typical personal credit card limit.

Your expenses don't match the rewards program that many commercial credit cards provide.

* You're not interested in obtaining credit to build the business.

* You're not the only one to take out an unsecured business loan in the near future.

Who can apply for a Corporate Credit Card?

The first thing you must meet to be eligible to get a business credit card is having a business. If you don't possess at least one form or business entity, would it suggest that you're not eligible for a corporate credit card?

The truth is there is no. You are able to qualify for a credit card for business even if you're just looking for the benefits these cards offer.

The reason is straightforward: there's no definitive definition of what is a "business" is actually. It could be anything from selling merchandise at a flea marketplace or operating a company with over 100 employees in it. It doesn't matter at all whether your experience in business involves the setting up of an outdoor lemonade stall outside of your house.

If the revenue you earn through your work can be considered to be business-related revenue and you can be able to use the business credit card. Whatever the case, the company will continue to scrutinize your personal credit data to determine if you've got the necessary information to meet the requirements the card will have.

Different types of business cards

There are many business cards you could apply to. They are all the same in terms of specifications and functions but come with certain features which make them suitable for many scenarios. The following are the features:

1. Businesses Credit Cards

They are the standard credit card, and function much the same way as personal cards. They come with a credit limit which determines the amount you can spend on your card per month, as well as the amount you are charged.

When your card is charged with charges, you're legally bound to pay for the cost each billing cycle. It doesn't mean that you need to pay it immediately in full, as you are able to pay the amount in installments. But, it will mean you'll carry the balance month after month i.e. you'll need to pay interest until you settle the debt.

But, it does allow the small amount of financial cushion that small-scale business owners can be reliant on during difficult times.

2. Credit Cards for Business

As with the standard business account, the charge card serve the same purpose as credit cards used for personal use. But, they are different in regards to credit limits, since, generally there are none.

Charge cards come with what is known as"shadow" limit "shadow" limit that tends to be greater than the majority of credit card limits. These limits can be adjusted based on the needs of the card holder. They may also be altered based on the frequency of use for your card , as well as the general status in your credit record.

However, there's an issue: if you go over the limit could cause that your bank account be frozen. You cannot also keep the balance monthly to monthly basis. You'll be required to pay for the balance at the full amount each time you bill.

This card is only recommended for those who have complete control of the spending patterns of their household. If you are able to spend only on the amount you can pay for, this card may be right for you.

3. Secure Business Cards

This card is perfect for small-scale businesses that have no personal credit, or no credit whatsoever. It's credit card that builds credit, specifically designed for business owners.

The procedure is easy. When you apply for the card, you will be required to make a deposit of a certain amount. This can be between $2,000.00 or $5,000.00 depending on the card's issuer and the card.

The amount you have set up serves as your credit line, and you could use it to cover any expenses that is related to your business. Whatever way you choose to use it, every payment to the amount will be made through the agency that issued the loan to credit.

So, your business can grow its credit in the course of one year. It is important to remember that only timely payments are recorded. Every payment that is missed will be considered a derogatory mark and will sabotage the goal for the credit card.

How to Get A Corporate Credit Card

The process of getting your company's credit card is actually quite easy. The procedure is similar to obtaining an individual credit card. But, there are some different details you must provide to the company that issued the card. Because this is a business credit card, it is obvious that the company is going to request details about your company.

This application will have questions such as:

Legal name for the company

* Address

* The kind of industry it is part of. Certain industries are considered to be high-risk and have high-maintenance, which may impact the acceptance of your application.

* The form of the business, regardless of whether you're an sole proprietorship or partnership, or an organization.

* The age of the company i.e. how many years it has been operating.

* The number of employees in addition to the structure of the organization.

* Annual income

* Estimated monthly expenses as well as other finance-related items.

It is entirely dependent on the institution what information they would like from you. To make it simpler on your end it's best to search for the details you have to provide and then make your documentation and answers in advance.

What Do You Need To Do To Secure An Instant Approval

At the final moment, it's entirely up to the bank or other comparable financial institution determine whether or not they will approve your request for a credit card for your business. In order to make them quickly decide whether to accept your application There are a few things to consider before you apply:

1. Are you a business owner?

While you don't have to be a part of a company to be eligible for a corporate credit line, having one will enhance your chances of being able to secure one. The lender will most likely want to ensure that the credit or money you are able to secure with the card is put towards the actual operation. A way to show that you are an established business is to obtain an Employer's Identification Number (EIN) from the Internal Revenue Service as well as opening a business bank account.

2. Have a good to excellent Personal Credit Score

Your credit score will affect the way your application is likely to be evaluated. The lender must be sure that you are able to meet the requirements of the credit card.

To do this, they will do a thorough lookup of your credit history , and then look at any mark that was made about your financial transactions. What a creditor will consider is different from the other, but it's certain that applicants who have a track record of timely payments, high credit utilization rates and little or no negative marks are more likely to be more likely of being approved for their application.

What kind of transactions can the business Credit Card Be Used for?

There isn't a hard and fast rule of thumb for what and how to utilize your company's credit cards. It has the same functions as your typical credit card albeit with a larger credit limit and a few more restrictions/obligations on your part.

The focus, therefore it's not about which business credit card is the most appropriate, but rather on how you can optimize the use of your credit card and minimize the risk that it brings. For that there are some guidelines to remember.

1. Be Certain That Everything is Strictly in Business

Even if you're as a sole proprietorship, you should resist the temptation to use your credit card on personal issues. Making sure your business expenses are separate from your personal ones is a method of keeping track of your expenses, and also claim deductions during tax season. around.

If you permit staff to make use of the card provide guidelines on what is considered an expense for business. Implementing a procedure that requires employees to obtain approval prior to using the card and provide receipts is a great way to enforce accountability while limit the card's usage.

2. Set a Rule of Law

If you run an organization, it is likely that your employees will want to use the card. This is an opportunity to develop a policy regarding how to utilize the card.

Conclusion

As you've read that after the fall there are many ways to recover and get back into the credit. The issue that people confront when recovering is the nagging desire to go back to the same old routines. The thought that goes through your mind when contemplating making a purchase could be "Just once, I'll make a purchase using the credit card I have." Don't do it! This is the only way the previous self is allowed to charge again.

You've put in a lot of effort to settle and restoring your standing to the level you have today. It took time, but you're now at a point where you're no longer in a state of worry.

Maintaining your finances and accounts to a good order can be a routine that lasts for the rest of our lives. When it comes to dieting, it's a lifestyle change and the same is true for our financial situation. You will not only feel better about yourself through a change in your lifestyle and staying within your budget However, you also be an example for your family and other friends. Children learn to manage their parents' finances effectively. If you're a successful financial planner, your children will be as well when they're grown. Even if you've had difficult times, your kids will be able to see the choices you made for yourself.

The most important thing you can learn in this guide is ensure you've got a budget in place. This is something you should put a lot of importance on. It's when you're out of reach and not being aware of what's going on into and out that's going lead you to a dead end. This is a new method that is worth studying.

New laws are always changing and regulations. Be aware of any changes is a part of the new financial lifestyle. Be sure to read the documents that the banks and credit card companies are releasing. Even the small print that is difficult to look through is full of information that can modify your credit conditions and even save you money.

You shouldn't be too cautious about your identity in the present day world. It's sad that we have to look for unscrupulous individuals who seek to take advantage of our identities and utilize them to harm others in every way. Always be vigilant to protect yourself as well as your kin's identity.

Give your self a pat the back. You're worthy of this. You're back on the right track today and have learnt from the mistakes you made. Now is the time to begin building towards your goals.

www.ingramcontent.com/pod-product-compliance
Lightning Source LLC
Chambersburg PA
CBHW050402120526
44590CB00015B/1793